Speaking Truth to Power

POLICY, ADMINISTRATIVE AND INSTITUTIONAL CHANGE

Series Editors: Giliberto Capano, *Professor of Political Science, Scuola Normale Superiore, Italy* and Edoardo Ongaro, *Professor of Public Management, The Open University, UK*

Change is the main explanatory challenge for the social sciences. Stability and persistence are simpler to understand and explain than change; at the same time, change is not separated from stability, and, from this point of view, any approach to change (in whatever field) should be able to account for both 'constancy and change'.

Change is of significance, both for explanatory reasons, and from a more normative/prescriptive standpoint. To address, lead, control and implement change is a key task for policy-makers who, to adjust to or improve reality, constantly strive to cope with reality through designed changes in the institutional structure, in the organizational and processual dimensions of public administration, and in the governance arrangements of policies.

Following up on the above premises, this series is aimed at publishing books offering new, original, and enlightening views on change in action. The series is committed to overcoming the borders between scholars in public policy, public administration and management, and political institutions. Change happens at the crossroads where political institutions, policies and public administrations constantly interact and influence each other.

This broad perspective is highly relevant and innovative, both from the scientific and the applied perspective. The series, with its multi-dimensional and multi-theoretical commitment, is designed to offer significant information and high-quality practical knowledge for both scholars and policy-makers alike.

Titles in the series include:

Public Governance Paradigms
Competing and Co-Existing
Jacob Torfing, Lotte Bøgh Andersen, Carsten Greve and Kurt Klaudi Klausen

Policy Change and Innovation in Multilevel Governance
Arthur Benz

Speaking Truth to Power
Expertise, Politics and Governance
Benjamin Ginsberg and Collin Paschall

Speaking Truth to Power

Expertise, Politics and Governance

Benjamin Ginsberg

David Bernstein Professor of Political Science, Johns Hopkins University, USA

Collin Paschall

Assistant Director of the Center for Advanced Governmental Studies, Johns Hopkins University, USA

Cheltenham, UK • Northampton, MA, USA

© Benjamin Ginsberg and Collin Paschall 2022

All rights reserved. No part of this publication may be reproduced, stored in a retrieval system or transmitted in any form or by any means, electronic, mechanical or photocopying, recording, or otherwise without the prior permission of the publisher.

Published by
Edward Elgar Publishing Limited
The Lypiatts
15 Lansdown Road
Cheltenham
Glos GL50 2JA
UK

Edward Elgar Publishing, Inc.
William Pratt House
9 Dewey Court
Northampton
Massachusetts 01060
USA

A catalogue record for this book
is available from the British Library

Library of Congress Control Number: 2022941192

This book is available electronically in the **Elgar**online
Political Science and Public Policy subject collection
http://dx.doi.org/10.4337/9781803927633

Printed on elemental chlorine free (ECF)
recycled paper containing 30% Post-Consumer Waste

ISBN 978 1 80392 762 6 (cased)
ISBN 978 1 80392 763 3 (eBook)

Printed and bound in the USA

To Sandy and Annie

Contents

List of figures		viii
About the authors		ix
Acknowledgments		x
1	Becoming expert on experts	1
2	Experts in the 21st century: Cassandras in the modern Troy	24
3	Crisis and decision-making	43
4	Speaking truth to bureaucracies	68
5	The truth is, using power is fraught with risk	85
6	Expertise and political conflict: a macroscopic view	103
7	Convincing the powerful of the truth	117
Index		125

Figures

2.1	Stylized illustration of prediction using regression modeling	32
3.1	Personality traits and tendency towards action	63
4.1	Number of FACA committees by agency, FY 2019	74
4.2	Proportion of representative FACA members by agency, FY 2019	74
4.3	FACA recommendations per committee by agency, FY 2019	75
4.4	FACA recommendations implemented by agency, FY 2019	76

About the authors

Benjamin Ginsberg is the David Bernstein Professor of Political Science and Chair of the Center for Advanced Governmental Studies at Johns Hopkins University. He is the author, co-author or editor of more than thirty books, including *The Fall of the Faculty*, *Presidential Government*, and *Downsizing Democracy*. Ginsberg received his PhD from the University of Chicago in 1973 and was Professor of Government at Cornell until 1992, when he joined the Hopkins faculty.

Collin Paschall is Assistant Director of the Center for Advanced Governmental Studies at Johns Hopkins University, where he teaches courses in social science research design and data analytics. Paschall received his PhD from the University of Illinois at Urbana-Champaign in 2018 and his law degree from the George Washington University Law School in 2011. He has been with Hopkins since 2019.

Acknowledgments

The authors are grateful to those who provided advice and guidance during the writing of this book. These include Gary Hollibaugh, University of Pittsburgh; George Krause, University of Georgia; Richard Waterman, University of Kentucky; Matthew Eshbaugh-Soha, University of North Texas; Dorothea Wolfson, Johns Hopkins University; and Jennifer Bachner, Johns Hopkins University. Dr. Paschall would like to thank Skip Paschall for his comments and feedback. At Edward Elgar, we wish to thank everyone who assisted in the production of this book, particularly Caroline Kracunas.

1. Becoming expert on experts

Decision-makers frequently find themselves required to make judgments that seem to depend upon specialized scientific, mathematical, or technical knowledge. When this happens, they often turn to experts – individuals with formal training, experience, achievements, and peer recognition in the field in question. Experts, in turn, often appeal to those in positions of power to support their ongoing work, framing it as an investment in information that can guide future decisions. In this way, it might appear that experts and decision-makers have a symbiotic relationship. Decision-makers want or need expert advice, and experts stand to benefit from offering such advice.

Today, indeed, the buying and selling of expertise is a highly organized enterprise. Decision-makers often solicit expert advice by turning to a specific expert or by publishing requests for proposals to the relevant community of experts. Bureaucratic agencies establish advisory committees of experts to help them make decisions. Not waiting to be asked, experts, for their part, often market their services directly to potential clients. Universities, think tanks, and consulting firms vie among themselves to secure some of the billions of dollars in grants and contracts offered by government agencies and private firms seeking expert advice, technical support, or the benefits of research and development. Experts working for universities frequently submit grant proposals to government agencies and private entities suggesting valuable research they might conduct in exchange for financial support. In the United States, for example, government agencies including the Department of Defense, the Department of Energy, and the National Institutes of Health, among others, support billions of dollars in scientific and technical research every year.

The partnership between decision-makers and experts, however, is not always a happy one. In the political realm, at least, the history of this relationship often has been fraught with mistrust and hostility. Decision-makers have rejected the advice of experts since time immemorial. In the Hebrew bible, the Book of Kings relates the story of Rehoboam, successor to Solomon. Rehoboam rejected the counsel of his father's experienced advisors and followed his own judgment. The result was a rebellion and the secession of the northern segment of the Israelite kingdom. More recently, experts have sounded the alarm on innumerable crises of the modern era, but all too often are frustrated by the sclerotic response of the government. And, of course, experts themselves are hardly perfect. To cite a recent example, as America's withdrawal from Afghanistan played out in the global media, experts vied with one another to blame other experts for having provided flawed advice.

One reason for the tension between the communities of decision-makers and experts is that those in power may not, at times, find truth to be politically convenient and will thus resist efforts to teach it to them. Moments of extreme crisis may offer some clarity, but generally power holders will gravitate towards confirmation and affirmation of truths that serve their political or other parochial interests. The bureaucracies responsible for most governance in the United States and other industrial nations are especially inclined to march to their own drummers and ignore or reject the advice of expert outsiders if it is inconsistent with either the preferences of the agency staff or those of their political principal. Conversely, experts are often not sensitive to the legitimate political concerns and dynamics of popular consent that occupy the minds of political leaders. Focused on a narrower cost-benefit or technical analysis of a given policy, experts may fail to understand the political steps that are required for the effective implementation of public policy. Without this shared understanding, experts and decision-makers find themselves at odds more than either side would ideally want as public policy challenges develop and demand response.

The importance of expertise goes beyond discrete problem-solving though. Competing forms and claims of expertise can help to determine the outcomes of struggles among rival political and social forces. With each generation, a new cadre of experts displaces those of the previous, a pattern that traces back to the beginnings of the scientific revolution, when the scientific experts deployed by the bourgeoisie proved their superiority to the priestly experts who served the aristocracy. The progressive evolution of expertise helps to bring down the old regime and pave the way for a new distribution of political and social power. Today, the global distribution of expertise and its digitalization threatens to do much the same thing. With an increasing dissatisfaction with the results of the neoliberal economic order and shattering of traditional cultural institutions, the experts who helped give birth to modern social and political institutions find their own legitimacy under attack by new experts supporting alternative visions of the political and economic order.

This book aims to guide the reader through the tangled relationship between truth and power, manifesting as the interplay between experts and decision-makers. Through a combination of careful observation and original analysis, we draw out the incentives and tensions that drive the relationship between these actors in society. We will review some of the history of expertise, consider the values of experts and decision-makers, and analyze what has succeeded and what has failed as truth and power have worked together and against one another, primarily in the United States but also drawing on international examples.

At its core, our claim is that while experts may attempt to remain politically neutral, expertise cannot be divorced from politics. It can only be understood and effectively leveraged to resolve public policy challenges if this reality is embraced and accommodated. There remains in some corners of American public discourse a notion, advanced perhaps most famously by Walter Lippman, that political decisions can and should be made by a cadre of technocrats who advise and guide political decision-makers.[1] Surely, no one could seriously argue that experts in public health, economics, and national defense should be ignored. But we aim to emphasize that expertise is not an unalloyed good, and too much faith in expertise can be quite naïve. At times, expertise can be a counterweight to power, but it can also be a weapon for the powerful. Appeals to expertise can be misguided, as decision-makers are understandably drawn to advice that confirms their predispositions and furthers their political agendas. Further, experts are not always adept at navigating treacherous political waters. Sometimes, it takes a special breed of expert to respond in times of crisis, and this is not always the kind of expert you might think. To improve decision-making, decision-makers need to become a bit more expert on experts.

EXPERTISE AND DEMOCRACY

Americans have a complex history and set of beliefs about the role of expertise in a democracy. American democracy emerged out of the intellectual heritage of the European Enlightenment, which during the 16th and 17th centuries saw the development of both Western liberalism as a political philosophy and the scientific method as an approach to understanding the physical world. In the future United States, many of the Framers, perhaps most notably Franklin and Jefferson, were known for their scientific interests as well as their republicanism. Indeed, the Framers understood that managing a complex new republic would require a degree of expertise. In Federalist 53, Hamilton or Madison (the authorship is unclear) describe the problem well. The Federalist author noted that "No man can be a competent legislator who does not add to an upright intention and a sound judgment a certain degree of knowledge of subjects on which he is to legislate." In a small state or single state, the issues which law must address would be narrow, but in a large nation, the issues are more diversified, and as such, representatives would need to acquire "extensive information" to govern effectively. The Federalists' solution to this was to allow for longer terms for legislators, whereby lawmakers would be able to gather greater knowledge about public issues over time.

The fact that legislators' requirement for knowledge in a diverse nation was a central consideration in the construction of the Congress indicates clearly how the importance of expertise was top of mind in the design of the American

Republic. Even so, there is also a strong undercurrent of anti-intellectualism, anti-elitism, and anti-expertise sentiment that runs throughout American history. With skepticism emerging from the citizenry and stoked by political leaders, reliance on expertise has sometimes been seen as antithetical to democracy, substituting the voice of the expert for the will of the people. The United States possesses an individualistic culture where personal rights and liberties are of great importance; as such, imposition of laws formulated by a select group of experts often faces stiff resistance. From a decision-maker's perspective, moreover, expertise is a form of power, and political decision-makers are often loath to surrender power to experts, particularly if they associate these experts with unfriendly political forces and hostile social strata.

This strain of anti-expert views in American political culture and history is often identified with Andrew Jackson and his followers. Jackson, who served as president from 1828 to 1836, famously derided the idea that expertise and experience were necessary qualities for government officials, saying, "the duties of all public officers are, or at least admit to being made so plain and simple that men of intelligence may readily qualify themselves for their performance."[2] For Jackson, this incredulity about the role of experts can be traced to his political tactics. "Jacksonian democracy" was based on the removal of the property requirements for male suffrage, and Jackson sought to capitalize on this by bringing in new, lower-class, less educated voters into Jefferson's Democratic Party.[3] Jackson used the bureaucracy not as a reservoir of technical or ministerial expertise, but rather as a party-building tool, using the "Spoils" system of corrupt dealings to stock government positions with partisan supporters. This put Jackson and his supporters in direct conflict with the business elite and "aristocracy" of the comparatively young nation. Jackson's dismissive posture towards experts matched Old Hickory's perception of his political interests.

In the late 19th and early 20th century, attitudes about the role of expertise in American life changed substantially, reversing course against Jacksonian thinking. As the United States became increasingly industrial and urban, labor conditions worsened, and at the time, there was limited if any protection again predatory wages or poor work conditions. There was also widespread concern about the perceived moral degradation of American society, perhaps most notably seen in the rise of the Temperance movement. Progressives relied on emerging theories about the social determinants of behavior to combat issues like drunkenness, poverty, and other public ills, and reformers made the importance of expertise and civic knowledge a major element in their political platform. Progressives argued, contra Jackson, that a modern, industrial society should be guided by scientists' growing understanding of technology, economics, and politics, and that citizens needed to develop the democratic competence to process such information.[4] This two-track approach to Progressive governance can be seen in the famous, so-called "debate" between Walter Lippmann and John Dewey, two of the most prominent Progressive thinkers in the United States.[5] Lippmann offered a critical take on citizens' capacity to comprehend public problems and reach consensus about solutions. His solution, in part, was to create bureaucracies of expertise which could guide public decision-making, removing some of the burden of governance from the fickle and poorly informed public. By contrast, Dewey saw the solution to citizen incompetence in reforming education to provide students with the skills needed to comprehend an increasingly complex society.

Of course, just as the Jacksonian distrust of experts was based upon political and social considerations, so the Progressive embrace of a technocratic, bureaucratic state guided by expertise had a political dimension. The latter half of the 19th century saw notable instances of political corruption, typified by the consolidation of power by political machines like that in Chicago or Tammany Hall in New York City. Supported by financial capital and industry, such machines were one of the targets of the Progressive movement. Reforms guided by experts targeting big business and political machines may have been aimed at defeating corruption, but this intention was entirely intertwined with the objective of unseating the dominant political powers of the time. Experts were, in a sense, coopted in a larger effort of political progressives to defeat their political foes.

Throughout the 20th century, the American state largely continued in the direction of greater Progressive reform and bureaucratic expansion. Jointly, the expansion of the social security system by the Franklin Roosevelt administration as a response to the Great Depression, followed immediately thereafter by the explosion of the national security apparatus during World War II and throughout the Cold War, served to drastically expand the size and scope of the federal government. Lyndon Johnson's Great Society established the federal government as the largest spender of health care dollars in the world. Critically, the Cold War period saw tremendous growth in higher education in the United States, with federal research and development dollars flowing to universities, making the United States the global leader in technological innovation. It was, of course, federal research money that led to the development of the Internet and the Information Age. Though briefly interrupted by the Reagan administration's emphasis on attacking the growth of the federal government, advocates for smaller government had limited success in curbing the growth of the state in the entire 20th century and into the 21st. Even during the administrations of George W. Bush and Donald Trump, there was no significant reduction in the size and scope of government. As we shall see, these administrations did engage in efforts to wrest control of the policymaking functions of the federal bureaucracy away from entrenched experts, but to the extent these efforts were intended to shrink the administrative state, they fell well short of their goals.

Most recently, the continuing tensions between Enlightenment thinking, Jacksonian democracy, Progressive reform, and expansion of the administrative state can be seen in controversies that arose around the COVID-19 pandemic. Before the pandemic even began, President Trump's largely working-class and rural and exurban political base was suspicious of elites and experts. Trump famously hung a picture of Andrew Jackson in the Oval Office, an homage to what his supporters portrayed as his political predecessor. Trump reveled in the disdain loaded upon him from America's upper-middle-class educated elite, many of whom regarded the populist president as racist, sexist, xenophobic, uncouth, and uninformed, to say the least. Not surprisingly, when COVID-19 began spreading through American communities in early 2020, educated Americans castigated Trump for ignoring expert opinion and demanded that he pay greater heed to the views of public health professionals. They seized upon criticism of the Trump administration from experts both within and without the federal bureaucracy. For example, much attention was given to the case of Rick Bright, a prominent epidemiologist, who said he had been removed from his federal post when he persisted in criticizing his superiors for failing to act quickly enough to produce medical equipment and for criticizing President Trump for touting the use of unproven therapies.[6] Trump, for his part, was suspicious of the government's medical experts, whom he seemed to regard as insufficiently loyal to his administration and insensitive to his political interests. In May 2020, the White House rejected guidance from the Centers for Disease Control (CDC) regarding the reopening of the nation's economy. The White House thought the CDC's recommendations were overly prescriptive, infringed on religious rights, and risked further damaging the economy.[7] Refusal to wear a mask and socially distance, as was recommended by experts, became a badge of honor and resistance to Trump and his followers, as much as an expression of hostility towards experts as it was an effort to maintain economic conditions that favored Trump in the upcoming election. It came as no great surprise to experts when Trump himself contracted COVID-19 just before the 2020 election.

It is important to point out that distrust of experts is not limited to Trump or to the federal level. Republican governors also echoed Trump's populist rhetoric. Ron DeSantis of Florida became a leading voice against vaccination and public health measures designed to control the spread of the disease. In 2021, DeSantis appointed to the office of Florida Surgeon General Joseph Ladapo, a controversial physician known for questioning the safety of coronavirus vaccinations,[8] and earlier in 2020 DeSantis allegedly fired officials in the Florida department of public health for refusing to "fix" virus-related statistics that might have supported continued quarantining.[9] Likewise, the Republican governor of Arizona, Doug Ducey, was dissatisfied with the advice he received from a team of University of Arizona and Arizona State University experts who had agreed to project the spread of COVID-19 in the state.[10] This academic modeling team projected a continuing and rapid increase in cases, especially if the state relaxed social distancing rules and allowed businesses to reopen. These projections were summarily rejected by the governor, who was accelerating plans to reopen businesses and had already declared that the state was headed in the right direction.

Trump and his Republican allies are heavily invested in attacking experts as a political strategy, but such distrust of experts does not follow a purely partisan pattern. New York Governor Andrew Cuomo, a Democrat, made critical comments about the value of advice from statisticians. The governor, anxious to make decisions that would mitigate the spread of the virus, was apparently hoping for certainties while statisticians could only offer a range of possibilities.[11] While perhaps less extreme than Trump's outright rejection of expertise, Cuomo's dissatisfaction with experts' uncertainty is only a milder refrain of the same theme.

EXPERT ADVICE: SUPPLY, DEMAND, AND MARKETS FOR IDEAS

Whether in the Jacksonian or Progressive eras or in the Information Age, misunderstandings and conflicts between experts and decision-makers could be characterized as disequilibria or mismatches between the supply of and demand for expert opinion. Just as some companies generate well-designed products that find no market, sometimes expertise that reveals truth fails to find an audience among citizens and political decision-makers. Conversely, politicians who want truth sometimes struggle to find it readily available, and may be deceived by low-quality research. Such mismatches often become visible when decision-makers complain about the advice they receive, and experts complain that their advice goes unheeded, either prior to a crisis or amid it. While examples of such incongruence were glaringly obvious during the COVID-19 disaster, many other mundane instances accumulate and characterize every level of political and bureaucratic process, in a variety of contexts, including such routine areas as program evaluation, management, and operational consulting and economic forecasting. In general, we see it as mostly likely for these kinds of mismatches to appear under several circumstances: (1) motivated information search, (2) heedless decision-makers, (3) black swan-style forecasts, and (4) an oversupply of advice.

Motivated Information Search

The first mechanism for a "market failure" for expertise to consider is motivated information search. Put simply, decision-makers do not like to hear or act on advice when the implications of that advice are counter to their pre-existing preferences. This tendency is readily seen in the area of program evaluation, for instance.

From the perspective of experts, program evaluation should generally be undertaken through the lens of evidence-based policymaking (EBPM). Through this methodology, programs can be evaluated for their cost effectiveness, assigned funding priorities based on their return on investment, and monitored to ensure that programs are achieving results commensurate with their goals and costs.[12] EBPM is an increasingly popular idea in contemporary policymaking, with advocates from across the political spectrum. In 2018, President Trump signed into law the Foundations for Evidence-Based Policymaking Act, a bill that implemented a variety of changes in how the federal government manages and uses data to guide its actions. This bill had broad bipartisan support, passing with the backing of 80 percent of the House of Representatives and with unanimous consent in the Senate. The support of lawmakers of both parties reflected broad support within the policymaking community, from both the conservative Heritage Foundation[13] and the liberal Urban Institute.[14]

While the language of EBPM seems to suggest a neat quantitative procedure allowing experts to offer objective advice to decision-makers, the actual process is not quite so simple. There are a number of significant obstacles to implementing such an approach. In some settings, the benefits of EBPM are very straightforward. Medical treatments based on random controlled trials are perhaps the gold standard for evidence-based action, as are some regulatory matters like automobile safety.[15] In a public policy setting though, assessing the effects of implementing a given policy usually goes beyond an objective measurement of costs and outcomes, invoking value judgments. One such setting is education.[16] Education invokes multiple instructional goals, like reading skills, science skills, math skills, or social development. Given constrained resources and time, it may not be possible to maximize all these goals simultaneously, so policymakers must make a choice about educational policy that very likely involves tradeoffs. EBPM may inform such choices, but the methodology does not always suggest a clear winner in such a situation where objectives conflict.

Another less subtle issue with EBPM is that important decision-makers and stakeholders are not above rejecting and discrediting evaluations that do not suit their own plans or preferences. One example here comes from the state level. In 1994, the state of Idaho created the Office of Performance Evaluation, an independent and nonpartisan agency of the state legislature. This office's purpose is to evaluate state projects selected by a Joint Legislative Oversight Committee (JLOC). The design of the committee is uniquely bipartisan in a state that is dominated by Republicans, with a requirement that members of the committee be equally represented by both parties. In an article written in 2019, the director of the evaluation office described the constant tensions that existed between his efforts to remain responsive to evaluation sponsors while protecting the evaluation's methodology, findings, conclusions, and recommendations from these selfsame sponsors' influences.[17] The state legislators who served on JLOC claimed to be seeking objective evaluations of state programs in such realms as education and healthcare, which constituted major items in the state budget. These evaluations would help them carry out their legislative responsibilities. At the same time, though, these legislators were sharply critical of program evaluations that called into question their own political agendas. In one instance, the chair of the state senate's education committee requested a study of workforce issues affecting public school teachers. When the evaluators published a report indicating concerns for the teachers, which may have elicited criticisms of the legislature's action, the same lawmakers that requested the studies immediately attacked the data-gathering effort.

This form of motivated reasoning and biased information-gathering among government officials also appears in the area of economic forecasts. Just as lawmakers are likely to attack negative evaluations of their actions, they are also prone to prefer forecasts that justify programs and policies from which they hope to derive political benefits. This process plays out routinely in the legislative process in Congress. As part of the Congressional Budget Act enacted in 1974, the Congressional Budget Office (CBO) provides "scores" for congressional legislation that estimate the expected cost of a bill. The CBO was intended to act as a counterbalance to the White House's budgeting authority, and as such it offers competing estimates of the budget impact of legislation that can be compared against those generated by the presidentially-controlled Office of Management and Budget (OMB) (formerly the Bureau of the Budget).[18] The establishment of CBO was responsive to the concerns that OMB is inclined to bow to political pressure from the White House and produce forecasts that overestimate future economic growth by a substantial margin. Such a picture gives policymakers a justification for increasing spending on popular programs or cutting taxes while avoiding unpopular tax increases or debt-financing.[19] As a result, it is common for the White House and CBO to offer competing budgetary projections, with the White House often offering an assessment that aligns with the political preferences of the administration. With these two competing budgetary projections, there is typically wrangling within and between Congress and the administration about the "true" cost of legislation, with politicians of course selecting which of the estimates is more favorable to their own stance. Interestingly, CBO forecasts, projecting lower rates of growth, appear to have been more accurate than OMB forecasts in recent years,[20] suggesting that Congress's economic forecasters have worked to check presidential ambitions by offering gloomier, and possibly more realistic, economic projections than those offered by the White House's own forecasters. However, it should be said that forecasting is an extremely challenging discipline that requires analytical choices about which there is genuine uncertainty. Regardless of which office is truly more accurate, the upshot is politicians are able to capitalize on the uncertainty created by these competing efforts. While they were not familiar with the technicalities of economic forecasting, the Constitution's Framers would be able to recognize in this process the continuing legacy of the checks and balances they built into the government.

Heedless Decision-Makers

In some situations, political decision-makers may seek to reject advice or courses of action that are inconsistent with their own interests. In others, decision-makers reject expertise and make poor decisions for more fundamental reasons having to do with their personalities and habits of mind. Some decision-makers may, for example, manifest a high degree of epistemic closure. That is, they may be so committed to a particular set of facts or some political or ideological or religious perspective that they process all ideas through the lens of that perspective and reject or reinterpret information inconsistent with it. In contemporary America, liberals and conservatives often accuse one another of epistemic closure. Epistemically closed decision-makers do not simply choose to refrain from acting upon some piece of advice. Rather, they simply cannot believe the validity of the advice and may, indeed, view an objectionable idea as an attempt to harm them, and react to it with some heat or even violence.

A famous example of such a decision-maker was Joseph Stalin, leader of the Soviet Union from the early 1920s until his death in 1953. Stalin had signed a mutual nonaggression pact with Adolf Hitler in 1939 and was fully committed to the idea that his shrewd diplomacy had prevented a possible German attack. Soviet military planners were not so confident.

Many were especially concerned that the major centers of Soviet industrial and arms production, including Moscow, Leningrad, Kiev, and Stalingrad, were near the nation's western borders, where a German attack might quickly overrun them. Experts, however, were afraid to communicate such concerns to Stalin, who was known to deal harshly with those who dared to question his ideas.

One Soviet planner, Boris Vannikov, the People's Commissar for Armament, had developed a detailed plan for the evacuation and reorganization of factories in secure areas east of the Ural Mountains in the event of a German attack, and had forwarded his plan to the Kremlin. Stalin did not wish to be contradicted and had Vannikov arrested on the charge of being a German spy. The unfortunate Vannikov was beaten and tortured by the secret police in Moscow's infamous Lubyanka prison. After the Germans attacked, Vannikov was released from prison and assigned to implement his once-discredited plan. Stalin assured Vannikov that his arrest had been the work of traitors who had now been dealt with, "most resolutely."[21]

Unwillingness to accept advice or even admit the possibility of error is also a characteristic of narcissistic personality disorder, which, unfortunately, seems to be particularly prevalent among decision-makers. Many commentators have observed that in both the corporate and political realms, individuals with narcissistic personality traits tend to compete for and ascend to high office. Psychiatry professor Jerrold M. Post wrote, "If we were to strip from the ranks of political figures all those with significant narcissistic personality traits, those ranks would be perilously impoverished."[22] Individuals with narcissistic personality traits are drawn to careers that put them in the public spotlight, contribute to their sense of importance and give them recognition and attention. Such individuals are helped in their quest for power and position because they attract followers who perceive them as decisive and charismatic. These followers derive much of their own self-worth from a relationship with an important and powerful figure.[23] Thus, it is not unusual to find important decision-makers who are convinced of their own superiority, suspicious of advice, and reluctant to admit mistakes. Among recent American presidents, Richard Nixon and Donald Trump come immediately to mind.

In some sense, the opposite extreme in personality can also represent a hindrance in listening to the advice of more seasoned experts. Instead of epistemic closure or malignant narcissism, a lack of intellectual discipline can be problematic. In their book on the use of history in political decision-making, Neustadt and May offer the story of the early days of Jimmy Carter's presidency.[24] Carter entered office hoping that the public would see his administration as a clear break from the Nixon–Ford years, offering a more "everyman" style of president. Carter also had an extensive agenda, aiming for comprehensive welfare, tax, and social security reform, to go along with a major legislative effort to combat the energy crisis. According to Neustadt and May, Carter's energetic attempts to kickstart his time in office were at least in part due to Carter's style of thinking. A former naval officer in the nuclear submarine fleet, Carter had what Neustadt and May identify as "a capacity for intense concentration on detail combined with a curious flightiness." As a result, Carter struggled to stay focused on issues and ran an administration that seemed frantic and "half-baked." Experienced observers of Washington knew that Carter did not understand the limits his proposals would face in surviving the legislative and executive machinery in Washington, DC, but Carter and his inexperienced staff were either unwilling or unable to receive that message. Subsequently, Carter's administration has largely been marked down as a failure in the historical record.

Of course, some decision-makers are heedless not because of patterns of mind but, instead, find it hard to understand expert advice because of cognitive impairment. Henry VI famously sat under a tree singing to himself during the 15th century Battle of St. Albans as troops loyal to him sought to outmaneuver the king's Lancastrian foes. In this vein comes to mind President Harry Truman's quip on the firing of General Douglas MacArthur in 1951 for, despite presidential orders, failure to pay heed to intelligence warnings of an imminent Chinese attack on American forces in Korea. After dismissing the general, Truman remarked, "I fired him because he wouldn't respect the authority of the President. I didn't fire him because he was a dumb son of a bitch, although he was, but that's not against the law for generals. If it was, half to three-quarters of them would be in jail."[25]

The Menagerie of the Future: Black Swans, Birds in the Bush, and Golden Geese

Aside from having leaders with significant personality or cognitive impairments to following expert advice, a third reason that decision-makers often ignore or reject experts is a set of common misperceptions about the future. All of these are related to having a poor grasp of probability and each has an avian nickname: black swans, birds in the bush, and golden geese. Of these, most in vogue in current literature on forecasting and expertise is the black swan. Popularized by Nassim Nicholas Taleb, black swans are events that are so improbable and unprecedented as to have been outside the realm of regular expectations but nevertheless have an enormous impact when they take place.[26] Taleb seems unclear as to whether such events are inherently unpredictable, or merely so improbable that they are usually not predicted.[27] A number of well-known events that Taleb calls black swans, however, were not only predictable but were actually predicted. The problem, though, was that expert advice went unheeded by decision-makers because the event seemed too unlikely to justify the expense of taking action or so improbable as to hardly even merit discussion. Experts attempting to convince decision-makers of the imminence of black swan events are more than likely to become modern-day Cassandras, doomed by the gods to accurately predict the future without ever being believed. This is the thesis of journalist Michael Lewis, who identified several lower-ranking public health officials who tried to alert upper-echelon officials at the CDC and other state and federal health agencies to the imminence of a major epidemic.[28] Their advice was ignored in the case of COVID-19, and they were subjected to ostracism and reprimands for having the temerity to speak truths to which powerful officials did not wish to listen.

The same interpretation of black swans is consistent with the 9/11 terror attacks. Prior to 9/11, a well-respected security expert, retired U.S. Army colonel Rick Rescorla, was director of security for the investment firm Morgan Stanley, then headquartered at the World Trade Center.[29] Rescorla had studied the 1993 World Trade Center bombing, concluded that another attack was likely, and after studying the building's vulnerabilities concluded that the next attack could involve the use of an aircraft crashing into the building. Rescorla recommended to company executives that Morgan Stanley, which occupied more than twenty floors in the south tower, leave the World Trade Center for safer office space in New Jersey. Executives declined to follow Rescorla's recommendation since, among other things, the company's lease did not end until 2006. Executives did, however, authorize Rescorla to institute emergency evacuation practices every three months to prepare for all eventualities including the plane strike he feared. These practices continued for several years even though some company officials found them intrusive and unnecessary.

Of course, on September 11, 2001, the attack predicted by Rescorla came to pass. As they had practiced, more than two thousand Morgan Stanley employees followed Rescorla down a stairway from the 44th floor of the south tower to safety. Rescorla himself perished when he returned to search for stragglers just before the building collapsed. Morgan Stanley executives had not completely dismissed Rescorla's warnings and had, indeed, taken some precautions in response to their head of security's advice. However, the seeming improbability of the event did not, in their view, justify the expense of moving the company's headquarters.

Another of Taleb's black swan events, the 2007–08 financial crisis, was also predicted by financial and economic experts who could not convince decision-makers to act. In some instances, decision-makers could not believe that well-established financial practices could have the ruinous consequences predicted by concerned economic and fiscal experts. In other instances, important decision-makers were deriving significant profits from questionable and risky practices and were unwilling to make changes. Take the case of the Federal National Mortgage Association (FNMA), generally known as Fannie Mae. Fannie Mae is a government-sponsored enterprise (GSE) established by Congress in 1938 to create a secondary market in residential securities. Access to this secondary market where mortgages can be resold encourages banks to make loans available to home purchasers. Helped by the widespread, albeit false, belief that Fannie's securities are backed by the full faith and credit of the U.S. government, investors watched with equanimity over the years as Fannie engaged in several profitable but quite risky business practices.[30]

These kinds of business practices led directly to the 2007–08 financial crisis, an outcome that no one would have wanted. Even so, the warnings had already been made at the highest levels of business and government. Nye Lavalle, a well-known investor advocate and activist, released a report in 2000 at the National Consumer Law Conference warning about the dangerous and predatory lending practices of several of America's major Wall Street firms and banks.[31] Nye had purchased single shares of stock in Fannie and the Federal Home Loan Mortgage Corporation (FHLMC, known as Freddie Mac), and he pieced together the outlines of the coming crisis years ahead of time, even sharing these results with the head of the Security and Exchange Commission at the very end of the Clinton administration. Lavalle's investigation also yielded evidence of "sham" pleadings filed by attorneys for Fannie and Freddie and fraudulent operations of the nation's mortgage registry system.[32] In 2004, federal investigators reviewed Lavalle's charges and found that Fannie's securitization, foreclosure, and legal practices were all problematic. CEO Franklin Raines was forced to step down and Fannie was compelled to restate its earnings, reducing them by some $9 billion.[33] Yet even so, the damage had already been done, and not enough was done to improve mortgage practices. In 2007, the collapse of the mortgage market, abetted by shady financial dealings, led to a financial crisis and a world-wide economic contraction. Major American financial institutions went bankrupt, and taxpayers were forced to bail out Fannie, Freddie, and other quasi-governmental corporations.

It is also worth taking note of what might be considered a subspecies of the black swan: the bird in the bush, an event that is generally acknowledged to be on the cards but seems to be sufficiently far in the future that experts find it difficult to motivate decision-makers to act today. One example is climate change. Almost all reputable scientific experts agree that man-made climatological changes pose possibly catastrophic threats to the global environment. It seems difficult, however, to motivate decision-makers in the United States and elsewhere to take serious action, such as sharply limiting the burning of fossil fuels, that might mitigate changes already underway. A large part of the problem is that catastrophe will take place sometime in the future. A recent United Nations (UN) report predicted serious consequences in 25 years. This is not exactly the distant future, but it is far enough off that decision-makers are reluctant to expend resources, incur costs, and mandate changes in behavior today to respond to a crisis that may be decades away. Decision-makers, like the rest of us, are inclined to discount the future.

Birds in the bush, moreover, will almost certainly produce political divisions. First, there are collective action problems. In the case of climate change, many nations hope that other nations will incur the current costs while all will share in the eventual benefits. India, China, and Brazil, for example, would like others to reduce pollution by diminishing their industrial production while they, themselves, continue to profit from high levels of industrial activity. Internal political divisions are important as well. Because catastrophe is in the future, domestic political considerations are likely to figure prominently in the here and now. In the United States, the Republican Party represents large and medium-sized industries whose costs would be increased by strict controls on carbon emissions and other forms of industrial pollution. The Democratic Party, for its part, represents non-manufacturing firms and not-for-profits and is also closely aligned with the regulatory institutions, such as the Environmental Protection Agency (EPA), that would gain in power, staffing, and budgets from stronger efforts to inhibit climate change. Hence, this issue has produced sharp domestic splits. Note that the Democratic Obama administration negotiated American participation in the Paris climate change agreement while the Republican Trump administration pulled America out of the agreement. The Democratic Biden administration subsequently renewed American participation in the Paris accords. Whatever experts think, action on climate change seems unlikely until decision-makers see a more imminent catastrophe.

Of course, a reason decision-makers are cautious in responding to birds in the bush is that experts make mistakes, and decision-makers latch onto predictions that can be framed as incorrect. A UN official reportedly warned in 1989 that global warming would wipe nations off the face of the earth by the year 2000 if climate change was not promptly addressed.[34] The same expert declared that global warming could raise the earth's temperature by 1 to 7 degrees by 2019. The actual increase has been about one-half a degree. Other experts have predicted imminent ice ages, the extinction of most animal species, and a host of other disasters. Perhaps these predictions are designed to impart a sense of urgency to the discussion of climate change. The result, however, may be to justify further discounting of the future on the part of many decision-makers. Experts must be careful not to give politicians room to misinterpret such statements.

Black swans are allegedly unpredictable cataclysms, and birds in the bush are widely predicted events in the future that seem too remote to be actionable. There is a third cousin in this genus to consider though: the golden goose. Occasionally, what comes out of the blue is an opportunity rather than a catastrophe. Opportunities, though, are not always easily recognized or even perceived by the untrained eye. Even when experts try to signal opportunities, decision-makers and the wider community of experts are sometimes too slow to accept a gift horse.

One important example is the case of smallpox vaccination. For centuries, smallpox was a scourge, killing millions of people. By the 18th century, inoculation was an established procedure, involving implanting dried smallpox scabs or pus under the skin of a healthy person.[35] Even so, it faced opposition – some American colonists considered intentionally infecting another person with smallpox to be a violation of the Sixth Commandment.[36] Benjamin Franklin and Thomas Jefferson were both proponents of the vaccine, but they faced significant public opposition.[37] When Edward Jenner first attempted to publish results of his experimentation with the cowpox vaccine, his results were in fact rejected by the Royal Society, and it took time for the expert community to coalesce in support of Jenner's discovery.[38]

A more recent example is the slow development of artificial intelligence (AI) algorithms. As digital computers became practical (if expensive) in the first half of the 20th century, a flurry of theorizing emerged from the mathematics and psychology communities about the potential for replicating "human" mental processes through computational methods. In 1958, Frank Rosenblatt of Cornell University pioneered the use of the "perceptron" as an early form of a neural network, an AI algorithm.[39] However, subsequently, MIT researcher Marvin Minsky wrote disparagingly of the promise of Rosenblatt's algorithm. In 1969, Minsky and Seymour Papert wrote an influential book that effectively ended research on the perceptron, kicking off an "AI winter" that arguably put back research twenty years.[40] It took a new generation of scholars to recognize that Minsky and Papert's analysis was incomplete, and in fact a solution to the issues they raised had already been invented. Today, artificial neural networks building on Rosenblatt's work are at the forefront of AI, and at the heart of many of the developments of the modern AI revolution. Like vaccines, the promise of neural networks went unrecognized because of internal debate within the community of experts.

An Oversupply of Advice

A final cause of severe mismatches between the supply and demand for advice is an oversupply of advice. The problem of oversupply has two dimensions: diversity and quality. With respect to the first of these, many people including decision-makers do not do well when they are overloaded with different choices. Experimental studies suggest that most individuals can become paralyzed and unable to act when confronted by too many options. In effect, the opportunity costs of any action become too great if a decision-maker is forced to choose among many apparently plausible courses of action.[41] In one study of employee participation rates in plans offered by the Vanguard Group, a large investment management company, researchers found that as the number of plan options increased, the rate of employee participation decreased.[42] For every ten options added to the plan, employee participation decreased by 1.5 to 2 percent. Relatedly, a recent study of baseball umpires showed that umpires tire of making decisions about strikes and balls over the course of a game, depleting their budget of attention and leading to errors as the game progresses.[43]

These dynamics effect elites and members of the mass public when they are trying to act under pressure. When offering advice, experts seldom offer only one path forward. Even when experts agree on basic scientific or technical questions, they often disagree on the next step. What should be done in light of this knowledge?[44] Both governmental and corporate decision-makers along with ordinary citizens are usually offered many options by many different experts. On the one hand, a multiplicity of experts can be a good thing, perhaps reducing the chance that some important perspective will be missed. At the same time, however, an oversupply of expert advice can also have deleterious consequences. Confronted with too many possibilities, advisees can succumb to paralysis and do nothing or, instead, conclude that the experts are confused and divided so they may as well do as they please. This is what played out in the first months of the COVID-19 pandemic with respect to mask-wearing. In the early days of the pandemic, experts provided labile and conflicting advice from various experts on such matters as the value of face coverings in preventing the transmission of the coronavirus. Many citizens took no action or concluded that it was best to simply decide for themselves.[45] Once that impression set in among citizens, aligned political leaders adopted the same fragmented approach, and an incoherent public policy followed.

Expert disagreements can pose one set of problems. Another set of issues can be spawned by too much expert agreement – that is, a lack of diversity of opinion. Experts, like other individuals, can be susceptible to a herd mentality in which members of a field reach some consensus, refuse to consider alternatives, and ostracize those who disagree. Sometimes, this rejection of alternative viewpoints can have negative consequences in the long term. In the case of the 2020 COVID-19 pandemic, after a short period of confusion leading public health experts almost unanimously recommended that schools be closed, businesses shut down, and social distancing requirements imposed. This advice was countered by a number of other well-credentialed experts, some coming from other fields, who questioned the need for these measures. Some of the outsiders attacked the projected course of the pandemic, arguing the cost of uncontrolled spread would not be as dire as public health officials suggested.[46] Others made a different argument, asserting that the long-term costs of prolonged shutdowns would extend to other areas, creating tradeoffs that might be unacceptable to many. Perhaps, these other experts warned, citizens would resent extended intrusion of government in the private sphere, and communities be angered by school and business closures.

On the public health front, the interlopers who argued that the pandemic would not be as severe as predicted appear to have been wrong. The pandemic was a global calamity, with millions of deaths. However, it must be said that the iron-clad consensus of public health experts may have led them to underestimate the second-order consequences of strong public health measures. Ultimately, the severe measures to control the pandemic were not successful in stamping out the virus. Waves of cases continued, while trust in public health experts weakened. Experts came to be viewed by some corners of public as dictating severe societal tradeoffs. Through this process, public health policy came to be deeply politicized, arguably reducing the power of experts in future crises.

It is difficult to know how experts should have calibrated their advice and what would have been the optimal policy response to the pandemic. However, the example of COVID-19 does illustrate the broader point: often, when new problems arise, communities of experts are resistant to semi-outsiders with less invested in a particular field's perspectives.[47] Failure to consider alternative perspectives increases the possibility of miscalculation and overlooking second-order consequences of policy alternatives.

Diversity of advice can be a good thing, but it must be added that sometimes the issue is not about the range of expert opinions and the value of having well-informed opposing viewpoints. Sometimes, advice that experts receive is just uninformed or, even worse, offered in bad faith. In the United States, this issue is especially serious because of the role of think tanks and advocacy groups in the policymaking process. "Think tanks" is an informal term for a broad class of nonprofit organizations that operate as policy-centered research organizations. Think tanks specialize in translating technical knowledge into recommendations for executive and legislative action, making them "boundary organizations" that operate at the confluence of communities of outside specialists and government actors.[48] Generally, think tanks became prominent in the Progressive era, with important examples like the Brookings Institution and the Carnegie Endowment for International Peace established during this period.[49] In the ensuing century, think tanks have become essential to the policymaking process in Washington and at the state level.[50] Basically, think tanks and policy institutes have become more successful than research universities in promoting, disseminating, and securing media attention for the opinions of their staffers.

Providing policy relevant information to decision-makers is, in the abstract, a good thing. However, think tanks in the modern era cannot always be described as objective actors. As McGann describes, many think tanks are thinly veiled advocacy organizations whose efforts are obviously directed at supporting an ideological and political agenda. The conservative Heritage Foundation and the progressive Center for American Progress typify this model, with both organizations operating essentially as shadow administrations for Republican and Democratic lawmakers. Beyond obvious partisan allegiances, think tanks are often "financially vulnerable" organizations that are reliant on industry support or even foreign sources of funding.[51] Foreign support for think tanks is of special concern in the context of U.S. foreign policy, and there are proposals from both liberal and conservative groups to require greater transparency in this setting.[52]

The result is often that what is taken for expert opinion does not actually represent the views of the nation's best qualified experts, generally, albeit not always, to be found in top research universities. If we focus on the realm of climate change as an example, we can see the inexpert character of many putatively expert reports published by think tanks of all political stripes. Take a recent Manhattan Institute report entitled "Overheated: How Flawed Analyses Overestimate the Costs of Climate Change."[53] The author, a senior fellow at the Manhattan Institute, is an attorney, with a law degree from Harvard University. The report criticizes climate studies as relying solely on statistical analyses of the effects of temperature variation. The report states that it explains the technical details of why these studies lead to incorrect conclusions, as statistical analysts are missing the bigger picture. It purports to review in detail two reports, one from a research consultancy called Rhodium and one from the EPA. Both reports forecast dire warnings about the costs of climate change based on temperature studies. The basic thrust of the report is that these models are flawed because they do not incorporate the possibility of human adaptation to increased heat. In the author's view, this fundamentally undermines the usefulness of the temperature change model. The notable thing about this piece is that the author is neither a statistician nor climate scientist nor in possession of any training in any relevant field. The author also fails to reference much actual scientific research on the matters at hand. Similar problems can be found in recent expert reports from across the ideological spectrum, issued by organizations like the Heritage Foundation, the Center for American Progress, Third Way, and the Institute for Policy Studies.

To be sure, not all think tank reports are inexpert. Some are authored by properly credential experts who engage the appropriate scientific research. Academic research does make its way into some think tank work, but there are surprising disconnections. Authors who are distinguished experts may not have terminal degrees in their claimed field of expertise, or may lack technical training in the fields in which they work. Some think tank reports might accurately be characterized as curated aggregations of news clippings. In the think tank world, claims of expertise are, at times, being packaged and sold to the media and different government actors by non-experts.

JUDGING MURPHY'S LAW

Comedian Eddie Murphy once said, "The advice I would give is to not take anyone's advice." At different times, this seems to have been adopted by both the mass public and among elite decision-makers, at both ends of the ideological spectrum in the United States. This tendency is consistent with a long tradition of distrust of centralized institutions and elites that sits at the core of American political identity. This complements the fact that leaders are often stubborn and close-minded, while also being accountable to a population that distrusts authority and faces its own psychological and cognitive obstacles in assessing public policy problems. This is not exactly a recipe for evidence-based policymaking.

But the blame does not rest entirely on the side of decision-makers or their constituents. Experts have their pathologies as well. The institution of expertise in the post-modern age has given way to a commodification and diversification of expertise that has allowed the concept to take many forms, which serves to overwhelm and confuse decision-makers and the public. Experts are also not neutral actors in political processes. They seek out political power of their own, at the expense of both majority consensus and minority objections. Narrowly focused on problems within their ken, some experts are not ideally positioned to make value judgments for society more broadly or build popular consent for costly individual sacrifices for the greater good.

This friction is the basis for our investigation in the chapters to come. To learn more about expert advice and its role in our society, we will evaluate the cutting edge of expertise for the Information Age, take a historical view of expertise in American society, and consider the deeper values and hidden assumptions that animate the operation of expertise in American life. What emerges, we hope, is a more accurate and even-handed assessment of expertise than what is typically portrayed in the modern media environment. As we will see, expertise is of great value, but it is not an omni-beneficent force emanating from university campuses, think tanks, or technocratic bureaucracies. Relatedly, while ignorance of expertise is a troubling pattern, uncritical adherence can lead to deeply problematic outcomes, both practically and morally. Our goal in the following chapters is to raise awareness of these tradeoffs, towards the goal of improving, or at least clarifying, the ongoing dialogue between truth and power.

NOTES

1. Lippman, Walter. 1922. *Public Opinion*. New York: Harcourt Brace.
2. *Messages and Papers of the Presidents*. 1899. Ed. James D. Richardson. Volume 2. Washington, DC: U.S. Government Printing Office, 449.

3. Feller, Daniel. N.d. "Andrew Jackson: The American Franchise." University of Virginia Miller Center. https://millercenter.org/president/jackson/the-american-franchise.
4. For a recent overview of the Progressive movement, see McGerr, Michael, 2010, *A Fierce Discontent: The Rise and Fall of the Progressive Movement in America*, n.p.: Free Press.
5. See, for an overview, Illing, Sean, 2018, "Intellectuals Have Said Democracy Is Failing for a Century. They Were Wrong," *Vox* December 20, www.vox.com/2018/8/9/17540448/walter-lippmann-democracy-trump-brexit.
6. Specter, Michael. 2020. "Trump's Firing of a Top Infectious Disease Expert Endangers Us All." *New Yorker* April 23. www.newyorker.com/news/daily-comment/trumps-firing-of-a-top-infectious-disease-expert-endangers-us-all.
7. Goodnough, Abby, and Maggie Haberman. 2020. "White House Blocks CDC Reopening Guidance." *New York Times* May 8, A1.
8. Balingit, Moriah. 2021. "New Florida Order Makes Quarantine Optional for Asymptomatic Children Exposed to Virus." *Washington Post* June 22. www.washingtonpost.com/education/2021/09/22/florida-student-quarantine-mask-controversy/.
9. NPR. 2020. "Florida Scientist Says She Was Fired for Not Manipulating COVID-19 Data." June 29. www.npr.org/2020/06/29/884551391/florida-scientist-says-she-was-fired-for-not-manipulating-covid-19-data.
10. Stanley-Becker, Isaac, and Rachel Weiner. 2020. "Arizona Halts Work of Experts Predicting a Later Peak." *Washington Post* May 7, A7.
11. Das, Arun Kristian. 2020. "Cuomo: What the Statisticians Couldn't Calculate About New Yorkers." *Fox5 New York* April 10. www.fox5ny.com/news/cuomo-what-the-statisticians-couldnt-calculate-about-new-yorkers.
12. Pew Charitable Trusts and MacArthur Foundation. 2014. "Evidence-Based Policymaking: A Guide for Effective Government." www.pewtrusts.org/en/research-and-analysis/reports/2014/11/evidence-based-policymaking-a-guide-for-effective-government.
13. Muhlhausen, David. 2015. "Evidence-Based Policymaking: A Primer." Heritage Foundation October 15. www.heritage.org/budget-and-spending/report/evidence-based-policymaking-primer.
14. Urban Institute. 2019. "Using Evidence for Improvement in the Foundations for Evidence-Based Policymaking Act." www.urban.org/events/using-evidence-improvement-foundations-evidence-based-policymaking-act.
15. Leuz, Christian. 2018. *Evidence-Based Policymaking: Promise, Challenges and Opportunities for Accounting and Financial Markets Research*. National Bureau of Economic Research Working Paper 24535. www.nber.org/system/files/working_papers/w24535/w24535.pdf.
16. Hammersey, Martyn. 2005. "Is the Evidence-Based Practice Movement Doing More Good than Harm? Reflections on Iain Chalmers' Case for Research-Based Policy Making and Practice." *Evidence & Policy* 1(1): 85–100.
17. Mohan, Rakesh. 2019. "I Didn't Know I Would Be a Tightrope Walker Someday: Balancing Evaluator Responsiveness and Independence." In Kylie Hutchinson, ed., *Evaluation Failures*. New York: SAGE, ch. 7.
18. Congressional Budget Office. N.d. "History". www.cbo.gov/about/history.
19. Krol, Robert. 2014. "Forecast Bias of Government Agencies." *Cato Journal* 34(1): 99–112.
20. Id.

21. Ginsberg, Benjamin. 2013. *How the Jews Defeated Hitler*. Lanham: Rowan and Littlefield, 22–23.
22. Post, Jerrold M. 2015. *Narcissism and Politics: Dreams of Glory*. New York: Cambridge University Press, ix.
23. Id. at 74–75.
24. Neustadt, Richard E., and Ernest R. May. 1986. *Thinking in Time: The Uses of History for Decision Makers*. Riverside: Free Press.
25. Lindsay, James M. 2012. "TWE Remembers: General Douglas MacArthur's Speech to Congress." *Council on Foreign Relations*. www.cfr.org/blog/twe-remembers-general-douglas-macarthurs-speech-congress.
26. Taleb, Nicholas Nassim. 2010. *The Black Swan: The Impact of the Highly Improbable*. New York: Random House. Some refer to the 2020 COVID-19 pandemic as a black swan, but the pandemic was, in one way or another, predicted by many experts. Public health measures, albeit insufficient, were certainly undertaken by most advanced, industrial nations. Pandemics, at any rate, are hardly unprecedented in human history. The 1918 influenza pandemic killed tens of millions and probably altered the course of World War I. As recently as the first half of the 20th century hundreds of thousands of children each year contracted poliomyelitis, often resulting in death or permanent paralysis.
27. Werther, Guntram Fritz Albin. 2013. *Recognizing When Black Swans Aren't*. Society of Actuaries. www.soa.org/globalassets/assets/Files/Research/Projects/research-2013-black-swan.pdf.
28. Lewis, Michael. 2021. *The Premonition: A Pandemic Story*. New York: W.W. Norton.
29. Stewart, James B. 2002. *The Heart of a Soldier*. New York: Simon & Schuster. See also: Stewart, James B. 2002. "The Real Heroes are Dead." *New Yorker* February 4. www.newyorker.com/magazine/2002/02/11/the-real-heroes-are-dead.
30. Thomas, Jason. 2013. "Fannie, Freddie, and the Crisis." *National Affairs* 17, Spring. www.nationalaffairs.com/publications/detail/fannie-freddie-and-the-crisis.
31. Dayen, David. 2016. "The Foreclosure Sleuth." *New Republic* June 29. https://newrepublic.com/article/134722/foreclosure-sleuth.
32. Morgenson, Gretchen. 2012. "A Mortgage Tornado Warning, Unheeded." *New York Times* February 4. www.nytimes.com/2012/02/05/business/mortgage-tornado-warning-unheeded.html.
33. McLean, Bethany. 2005. "The Fall of Fannie Mae." *Fortune* January 24. https://archive.fortune.com/magazines/fortune/fortune_archive/2005/01/24/8234040/index.htm.
34. AP Newswire. https://apnews.com/article/bd45c372caf118ec99964ea547880cd0.
35. Markel, Howard. 2011. "Life, Liberty, and the Pursuit of Vaccines." *New York Times* February 28. www.nytimes.com/2011/03/01/health/01smallpox.html.
36. Id.
37. Fessenden, Marissa. 2015. "Thomas Jefferson Conducted Early Smallpox Vaccine Trials." *Smithsonian Magazine* February 4. www.smithsonianmag.com/smart-news/thomas-jefferson-conducted-early-smallpox-vaccine-trials-180954146/.
38. Boylston, Arthur. 2013. "The Origins of Vaccination: No Inoculation, No Vaccination." *Journal of the Royal Society of Medicine* 106(10): 395–398.

39. Lefkowitz, Melanie. 2019. "Professor's Perceptron Paved the Way for AI – 60 Years Too Soon." *Cornell Chronicle* September 19. https://news.cornell.edu/stories/2019/09/professors-perceptron-paved-way-ai-60-years-too-soon.
40. Schuchmann, Sebastian. 2019. "History of the first AI Winter." *Towards Data Science* May 12. https://towardsdatascience.com/history-of-the-first-ai-winter-6f8c2186f80b.
41. Schwartz, Barry. 2005. *The Paradox of Choice*. New York: Harper.
42. Retirement Plan Advisory Group. 2020. "Too Many Choices: How Many Investment Options Should You Offer?" January. https://retirementtimesnewsletter.com/2020/01/14/too-many-choices-how-many-investment-options-should-you-offer/.
43. Archsmith, James E., Anthony Heyes, Matthew J. Neidell, and Bhaven N. Sampat. 2021. *The Dynamics of Inattention in the (Baseball) Field*. National Bureau of Economic Research Working Paper 28922. www.nber.org/papers/w28922.
44. Grundmann, Reiner. 2017. "The Problem of Expertise in Knowledge Societies." *Minerva* 55(1): 25–48. www.ncbi.nlm.nih.gov/pmc/articles/PMC5306236.
45. Sullivan, Adam. 2020. "Choose Your Own Experts." *Iowa Gazette* April 20. www.thegazette.com/subject/opinion/staff-columnist/choose-your-own-experts-20200420.
46. Brownstein, Barry. 2020. "The Tyranny of (Alleged) Experts." *American Institute for Economic Research* April 16. www.aier.org/article/the-tyranny-of-alleged-experts/.
47. Tilcsik, Andras, and Juan Almandoz. 2016. "When Having Too Many Experts on Board Backfires." *Harvard Business Review* August 29. https://hbr.org/2016/08/when-having-too-many-experts-on-the-board-backfires.
48. Medvetz, Thomas. 2012. "Murky Power: 'Think Tanks' as Boundary Organizations." In David Courpasson, Damon Golsorkhi, and Jeffrey J. Sallaz, eds, *Rethinking Power in Organizations, Institutions, and Markets*. Bingley: Emerald Group, 113–133.
49. Id.
50. McGann, James G. 2016. *The Fifth Estate: Think Tanks, Public Policy, and Governance*. Washington, DC: Brooking Institution Press.
51. Forward, Jacob. 2021. "Historians and Think Tanks: Lessons from the U.S. Marketplace of Ideas." History and Policy. www.historyandpolicy.org/policy-papers/papers/historians-and-think-tanks-lessons-from-the-u.s-marketplace-of-ideas.
52. Clifton, Eli, and Ben Freeman. 2021. "Restoring Trust in the Think Tank Sector." Quincy Institute for Responsible Statecraft. https://quincyinst.org/report/restoring-trust-in-the-think-tank-sector/. Clifton, Eli. 2021. "GOP Lawmakers Move to Expose Foreign Money in US Think Tanks." ResponsibleStatecraft.org. https://responsiblestatecraft.org/2021/03/19/gop-lawmakers-move-to-expose-foreign-money-in-us-think-tanks/.
53. Cass, Oren. 2018. "Overheated: How Flawed Analyses Overestimate the Costs of Climate Change." Manhattan Institute. www.manhattan-institute.org/html/overheated-how-flawed-analyses-overestimate-costs-climate-change-10986.html.

2. Experts in the 21st century: Cassandras in the modern Troy

The Greeks were guided by the Oracles. When in great duress, the Romans consulted the Sibylline Books. Nostradamus continues to grace the cover of tabloids from time to time. *Poor Richard's Almanack* included weather forecasts and astrological readings. Biff Tannen in *Back to the Future II* made his millions from sports gambling after acquiring a sports stats book from the futuristic world of 2015 and using it to make a series of winning bets starting in the 1950s. Though these examples are archaic or fanciful, they reflect a deep desire among the public and elites to understand what the future holds.

With the development of increasingly powerful technologies and methodologies, today the ability to predict the future with great accuracy seems tantalizingly within our grasp. Political analyst Nate Silver leveraged the statistical knowledge he gathered studying baseball statistics and started a cottage industry drawing millions of clicks focused on simulating and projecting election outcomes. Huge amounts of money are spent by investment banks to calibrate their portfolios in anticipation of future financial conditions. Actuarial models are at the heart of our public health and insurance systems. As we will discuss below, prediction is increasingly utilized by governments, in the spheres of both domestic and international policy. In the best-case scenario, prediction is a powerful tool for any institution, inside or outside of government. Accurate prediction and the application of expert knowledge can anticipate catastrophe and guide the efficient allocation of effort and resources. However, as with other aspects of the interplay between expertise and government, there is also much potential for misuse, abuse, and ignorance. Modern-day oracles can be simply wrong, or they may be Cassandras giving warnings that go unheeded by the Trojans among us.

In this chapter, we explore some of the opportunities and obstacles in this domain. To begin, we will review how prediction compares to gathering and leveraging other kinds of expertise. Then, we review some of the ways that predictions are made. In doing so, we provide a demystification of emerging methods for quantitative forecasting. We close with an assessment of the prospects for predictive governance.

DISTINGUISHING INTERPRETATION, INFERENCE, AND PREDICTION

In traditional academic disciplines, subject-matter experts most frequently engage with two tasks: interpretation and inference. The first of these involves assessing the qualitative meaning of events or data, creating conceptual constructs that help contextualize facts, events, or processes. Interpretation can help to resolve debates like what the criteria ought to be for characterizing a state as a democracy or what we should consider a just distribution of outcomes in a society. This kind of theorizing is at the heart of social science and many legal questions. To determine the meaning of abstract ideas like "equality" or "due process" requires an understanding of history, values, and the traditions of a society. While debates over these issues may be contentious, subject-matter experts are in arguably the best position to weigh in on these matters.

A second traditional skill of subject-matter experts is inference, which is attempting to determine "what causes what" in the world. Whether done through qualitative or quantitative analysis, this can be extremely challenging. At heart, all techniques of causal inference reduce to being tricks to get around the so-called fundamental problem of causal inference, which is that for any unit of observation that is subject to a phenomenon of interest, we are only able to see the outcome for that unit where it is actually subject to that "treatment" of interest. We cannot simultaneously observe that unit having not received the treatment. In more concrete terms, if a physician wants to know the effect of aspirin on headache pain, she can give a patient aspirin but is then only able to observe the patient having received the aspirin; she has no perfect basis for comparison with any other time, place, or person because she cannot both give and not give aspirin to the patient and observe the difference between these two outcomes.[1] In a public policy context, the same logic holds. If political decision-makers have an objective, like lowering the obesity rate, there may be a variety of interventions that have this intended purpose. For instance, perhaps taxing sugary foods would lead consumers away from such products. While this is a sensible prediction, it is in a technical sense impossible to access two worlds where a city, state, or country both implements and does not implement this sugar tax.

In the case of aspirin and in medical trials, the widely used approach to causal inference is the randomized controlled trial, in which participants who are perceived as good candidates for a proposed medical intervention are randomly assigned to either receive the treatment or be placed in a "control" group and given a placebo. In this setting, while no two individuals in the treatment and control groups are likely to be identical, the treatment and control groups can be, on average, statistically identical, and thus the difference between the average effect of the treatment on an outcome of interest and average outcomes for the control group can be fairly attributed to the experimental intervention.

There is increasing interest in implementing this "gold standard" of scientific inference in contexts akin to the sugary food tax. For instance, the General Services Administration (a large independent federal agency that is responsible for purchasing many goods and services for the U.S. government) has a bureau within it called the Office of Evaluation Sciences (OES). OES's mission is to engage in statistically and methodologically rigorous evaluation of the effectiveness of government services and processes. This includes using randomized control trials to test the effects of proposed programmatic actions, like the effectiveness of increasing the amount or changing the content of email communications with educational caseworkers on identifying homeless students. Many local and state governments have created similar offices, with the goal of improving and reducing the costs of government services.

Of course, randomization is not an option in many political or policy settings. Random assignment may be impractical, unethical, or impossible. Imagine, for instance, the problems that would come with intentionally randomly exposing children to known harmful chemicals as a method to infer the effect of exposure on academic performance. In such instances, researchers have to instead rely on a variety of creative statistical and econometric techniques to approximate the experimental setting. Researchers are making progress with these techniques, but they still fall short of the simplicity and easy-to-communicate approach of randomization.[2]

Causal inference is, in a sense, a specialized case of predictive analytics. By establishing causal relationships between variables, social scientists can make informed guesses about the future state of the world given a set of interventions. However, in other respects, prediction does not follow the same set of scientific procedures and has quite different objectives, making it a discipline in and of itself. Probably the single biggest difference between prediction and scientific inference is the role of explanation in both processes. For scientists, inference is a tool for explanation. Scientists want to understand the underlying mechanisms that drive action in the world, and to this end causal inference is a tool for theory testing. On the other hand, the single-minded predictioneer may not have any particular interest in understanding why a relationship between two variables holds true, or whether that relationship is robust across many different contexts. The emphasis in prediction is simply getting to the correct answer, regardless of the theoretical story at play. This is not to say that forecasters are completely uninterested in theory; it certainly is helpful to understand enough about the world to have an awareness of the facts on the ground and an intuition about "what goes with what." It may also be useful to have some interpretive expertise, as that aids them in developing intuitions about human or institutional behavior. However, at bottom it may be possible to make a good prediction without having the same thorough understanding of the underlying phenomena that would be the objective of more focused scientific inquiry. There may be multiple potential and plausible causal pathways that could lead one set of conditions to give way to the next, and the forecaster does not have to be exact about which of these is uniquely or jointly "responsible" for the future set of events. What is needed is some process that gets to the eventually correct prediction, and a good forecaster will have a track record of building such predictions.

Conceptual distinction aside, between interpretation, inference, and prediction, the most in-demand form of expertise in a governmental or public policy setting would be prediction. While interpretation and inference might be useful as rhetorical resources, hard-nosed realist politicians are likely to value most information that allows them to achieve objectives, whether in pursuit of personal gain or collective benefit. Shamans of the past may have concocted entirely incorrect theories about *why* the rains came down, but if they were able to predict with accuracy the auspicious times for planting, they were likely to preserve their own status and the survival of their communities. And while in the past these predictions might have been only roughly or intermittently accurate, in the ensuing few millennia the prospects for accurate prediction have improved.

METHODS OF PREDICTION

The last decade has seen tremendous growth in the interest accorded to forecasting in the public sphere. In pop culture, we can see this in the increasing interest in forecasting in sports, where the application of "Moneyball" techniques in baseball has revolutionized the sport – much to the chagrin of some fans and old-timers. Weather forecasting has also seen a surge in public interest, as forecasting models like the "Euro" and "GFS" models are publicly available for the scrutiny of amateur weather watchers. As mentioned above, politics too is included in this surge in interest, most commonly seen in the uptick in quantitative election forecasting.

While the interest in forecasting has existed since prehistory, arguably the last seventy years have seen greater progress in this area than in the preceding ten thousand. One way to characterize this progress is to describe it as the culmination of several major lines of research. A first category of inquiry has sought to better understand humans' capacity for rational individual reasoning and prediction. A second stream of work is focused on advances in quantitative and computationally aided human prediction.[3]

Behavioral Economics and Good Judgment

Since their emergence in the early 20th century, cognitive and social psychologists have made substantial efforts towards developing and testing theories of individual behavior, including research on people's ability to make "rational" decisions that result in their benefit, either individually or as part of a collective. In recent years, perhaps the most widely influential work in this domain is Daniel Kahneman's 2011 book *Thinking, Fast and Slow* (TFS).[4] TFS summarizes a research program going back decades spearheaded by Kahneman and his long-time collaborator Amos Tversky. After Tversky's death, Kahneman was awarded the Nobel Prize in 2002 in recognition for this work, though this stream of research has benefited from important contributions from numerous other scholars. The central insight of inquiry as summarized in TFS is that human thinking and judgment can be understood as a joint result of two cognitive systems, which Kahneman dubs "System 1" and "System 2." System 1 is a set of autonomous and mostly involuntary mental processes, like orienting to a sudden sound, disgust reactions, or reading simple texts. System 2, by contrast, is an effortful application of mental activity, dealing with more complex calculations than System 1. Common System 2 activities would include filling out tax forms, telling someone a phone number, or analyzing a complex argument. Human behavior emerges from the interaction of System 1 and System 2. System 1 is constantly scanning an individual's environment, creating what Kahneman calls "basic assessments" of stimuli as "good" or "bad." These impressions are passed along to System 2, and this process creates "intuitive judgments" about the people, places, and things around us.

Along with its review of System 1 and 2 thinking and psychological heuristics and biases, the third and perhaps most significant contribution of TFS is its review of prospect theory. Prospect theory is essentially the idea that people tend to view gains and losses in an unbalanced way. The theory describes how judgments about gains and losses are pegged to reference points that vary across individuals with context, and, further, how human decision-making is characterized by risk aversion, where potential losses (vis-à-vis the current reference position) are weighted more heavily in decision-making processes than gains.

An important conclusion of Kahneman's work is that through this process, humans are prone to significant errors in judgment and thinking. For example, following what he calls "the law of small numbers," Kahneman shows that people have a strong tendency to believe that small samples are necessarily illustrative of larger samples. If, for example, a person knows the economic conditions in his or her own community, they might tend to assume fallaciously that the conditions in another location are similar to their own. To use a sports analogy, commentators might believe that a certain player gets "hot" in a basketball game, even though more systematic analysis reveals that these purported moments of high performance are really nothing more than random statistical noise, with no discernible pattern. Kahneman describes several such heuristics and biases which are innate to thinking, and, on the whole, the work forces readers to question their assumptions about the rationality of much of human decision-making.

The natural implication of this research as pertaining to prediction is to cast doubt on the feasibility of accurate and useful predictions by individuals or even experts. Though Kahneman does provide some evidence suggesting that trained experts engage in superior reasoning and forecasting than do laypeople, they are simultaneously prone to other kinds of errors. For example, Kahneman finds that experts are vulnerable to what he calls the "planning fallacy," which is the tendency for even highly trained individuals to consistently overestimate benefits of actions and underestimate costs. This problem is especially severe in irregular or unusual environments without easily available points of comparison. In such settings, System 1 creates coherence where there is none and System 2 is usually not up to the task of rejecting it.

Yet even as Kahneman and his colleagues' research was raising doubts about the ability of individuals to leverage expertise in decision-making and prediction, a second line of research, spearheaded by Phil Tetlock, was focused squarely on the issue of prediction. As with Kahneman and Tversky's work, Tetlock's research emerges from a much longer research project designed to assess what traits and behaviors characterized individuals who are excellent forecasters. In his "Good Judgment Project," Tetlock recruited pools of expert participants to respond to questionnaires that asked them to make forecasts about future events. Given enough time, Tetlock and his colleagues were able to assess which forecasters were more accurate than others, and then they conducted detailed analysis to see what characteristics distinguished more or less accurate forecasters. Tetlock summarized his work in highly regarded books in the early 2000s: *Expert Political Judgement*,[5] which was aimed at an academic audience, and *Superforecasting*, co-authored with Dan Gardner and written for a general audience.[6]

Among other insights, perhaps the key distinction uncovered in Tetlock's research was a distinction in the cognitive styles of experts, dividing them into two groups that Tetlock called "hedgehogs" and "foxes." Hedgehogs are individuals with deep knowledge of a single topic or theoretical approach to problem-solving. Hedgehogs tend to be highly confident in their predictions. Foxes, by contrast, are more flexible thinkers that draw on diverse information sources and methods of thinking, and those in this category express greater skepticism towards their own powers of prediction. Tetlock characterizes foxes as being in a state of "perpetual beta" in reference to the unfinished "beta" stage of development of computer software.

The widely known takeaway from Tetlock's work is that subject-matter expertise was not equivalent with forecasting skill. Some subject-matter experts who did not operate as foxes or in a perpetual beta mindset performed quite poorly in forecasting challenges, worse than competitors who had the right approach to thinking but not the same level of deep substantive knowledge. Tetlock finds that the very best forecasters tend to be cautious, non-deterministic, open-minded, reasonably intelligent (though not exceptionally so), comfortable with numbers and probabilities, open to updating beliefs, non-ideological, and possessive of a growth mindset. Forecasters showed the ability to improve over time, presumably because they learned from errors. Many in the popular press took this as a condemnation of expertise, but this is a characterization Tetlock explicitly rejects. It is not that experts are not important in a society, or that expert knowledge is not helpful in forecasting. Instead, the point is different: forecasting is a specific skill that is best executed by people with certain traits and behaviors.

Technical Approaches to Forecasting

Between the two lines of Kahneman's and Tetlock's research, the reasonable conclusion to draw is that skill at prediction is not evenly distributed across the population, but with the right cognitive orientation, certain "superforecasters" are able to compensate for some of the inherent weaknesses of human cognition. It may be that some sages of centuries past were in a state of perpetual beta, and although their information sources may have been incomplete, they were able to distinguish themselves through their wisdom. Yet even as our formal understanding of this ancient tradition of informal forecasting has grown, it is increasingly complemented by an impressive suite of new analytical tools, promising advances in forecasting far beyond even the most refined human intuition. Here, we review two strains of these technological aids: forecasting based on game-theoretic modeling and forecasting based on statistical and artificial intelligence (AI) methods.[7]

Modern game theory's historical development is complex, but a good place to peg as the starting point is John Nash's famous work from the mid-20th century.[8] Nash came to prominence for his work on noncooperative game theory. In a nutshell, Nash and other scholars in this tradition advance the idea that individuals (and possibly, by extension, some organizations) act following a simple set of utilitarian rules, seeking to do what is in their own best interest given a set of choices of actions. So long as individuals can be understood as having ordered and fixed preferences across a set of possible outcomes, game theorists suggest that a mathematical function can be assigned to these individuals that reflects their preferences and preferred actions. With strategic players' preferences weighted, computational models can be developed that will predict the likely outcome of strategic scenarios, given these inputs. One important scholar in this tradition, Bruce Bueno de Mesquita, has written elegantly and persuasively about the power of this methodology to support good decision-making. Bueno de Mesquita came to prominence in the 1980s, using this approach to make predictions about the leadership of post-Khomeini Iran. In the time since then, Bueno de Mesquita has worked with the U.S. defense and intelligence communities as well as in private consulting, applying his methods to make predictions in support of strategic planning. Although he cannot provide the details of all his projects, Bueno de Mesquita credibly reports that his predictions have a 90 percent rate of success and are at least twice as accurate as the forecasts of well-informed and resourced subject-matter experts within the U.S. government.[9]

In addition to game theory, a second technical approach to forecasting is through statistical and "big data" computational methods. "Big data," "forecasting," "predictive modeling," and other terms are thrown around frequently in popular culture these days. Watching NFL football on Sundays, the average American sees advertisements for "Next Gen Stats" by Amazon that produce "power rankings" and win probabilities that change dynamically over the course of a game. Companies like Amazon, IBM, and many others claim that their new AI platforms will boost sales and productivity in almost every field. At the outset though, it is important to be clear about the terminology surrounding "big data" analysis. Our general advice is to ignore most of the terms, which are as much marketing hoopla as anything else. Phrases like "artificial intelligence," "statistical machine learning," and "deep learning" are not especially meaningful. These are general umbrella phrases that capture a wide range of statistical and computational tools. Broadly speaking, these terms are hierarchical – AI is the broad pursuit of computer software that mimics human judgment and cognition. Machine learning is a set of tools primarily aimed at prediction and classification. "Deep learning" is a particular technical approach used in machine learning processes that is conceptually derived from models of human cognition. The most important thing to take from the terminology is that all of it refers to methods for taking data and making predictions about the future based on those data, using a variety of statistical and computational techniques.

Putting terminology aside, a few relatively simple examples can provide an intuition about the processes being implemented in many AI contexts. A good place to start is a form of predictive modeling that should be familiar to anyone who took high school algebra but has been rebranded as "supervised machine learning." Supervised learning is the process of using data that connect known predictors and outcomes to forecast future outcomes based on new values of similar predictor data. To give a trivial example, imagine that you are interested in understanding the relationship between exercise and longevity. You might imagine that there is a positive relationship between these two variables – individuals that average more minutes of exercise per day at, say, age 30 should have a longer lifespan than individuals that are less active. You could easily plot these two variables on an x–y coordinate plane, and it would look something like Figure 2.1.

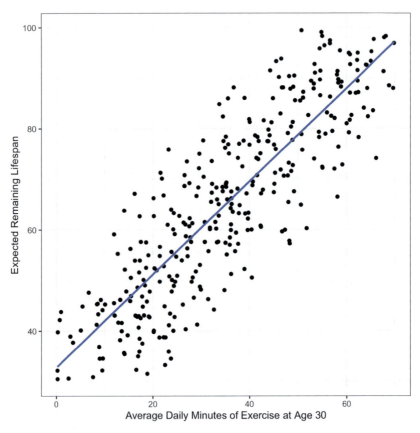

Figure 2.1   Stylized illustration of prediction using regression modeling

With this figure, if you were asked to predict lifespan based on the amount of exercise while young, you could probably make a reasonable guess. If you wanted to be more precise, you could use the line in the plot that has been generated with regression modeling – that is, the line with the minimum possible total distance from the line to each point in the cloud at each value on the x-axis. With this line, given any value on the x-axis, you can come up with a best-possible guess for a person's age at death, given the data available. This stylized illustration of regression modeling sidesteps a huge literature in statistics about the best procedures for making predictions or doing classification using supervised learning, but regardless of the exact method being used, the generalities of the process are the same – using data from the past about precursors and outcomes allows analysts to make guesses about future outcomes.

AI and predictive modeling have become more user-friendly with software developments and less expensive with reductions in the cost of computation, and now these technologies are applied in a huge array of business contexts. Governmental bureaucracies are of course slower to adopt innovations than the private sector, but there is great potential for the implementation of these tools in the public space. An interesting recent piece of scholarship published by Joan Timoneda and Erik Wibbels in the journal *Political Analysis* provides an example of how predictive modeling can be used to study trends in behavior. As an illustration, it is useful to review this work in some detail.[10] Timoneda and Wibbels's study focuses on using information about the frequency of searches for certain words in the Google Internet search engine and associating these data with protest activity around the United States. Google does not share the absolute number of searches for any given term in a time period, nor a term's relative frequency vis-à-vis other terms, but it does provide information about when a term reaches its peak frequency within any given time period, broken down at the by-hour level. This is published by Google as part of its "Google Trends" offering (GT). So, for example, if a researcher asked for GT data for the term "protest" between January 1 and January 2, 2020, GT would return a GT "index" value for 48 hours in that time period, and the hour with maximum frequency of searches for that term would be assigned a value of 100.

Timoneda and Wibbels based their analysis on a sample of protest actions in 130 metropolitan areas in the United States between January 2017 and May 2019. In essence (glossing over some important but technical details about data aggregation), Timoneda and Wibbels used these data to assign a numeric value that captures changes in search frequency for the term "protest" in every hour in the two months prior to and the one month after a protest began. Then, Timoneda and Wibbels created a second set of GT data for a sample of metro areas and dates in which no protest took place. Timoneda and Wibbels subsequently used these data to calculate the probability of a protest for every day in the two months prior to the protest event based on the values derived from the GT data, both in the cities where a protest took place and where a protest did not. Then, taking those results, Timoneda and Wibbels took the model (in other words, the mathematical formula that described the probability of protest action as a product of GT data about protests in days prior) and assessed how the calculated prediction of the probability of protest mapped on to the true pattern of protest initiation. Happily for the authors, they discovered that their model performed well, correctly predicting the occurrence of protests 85 percent of the time. Out of 130 "true" events, the model generated using the GT data correctly predicted the occurrence of the protest 110 times, and out of 133 "null" events (sets of GT data around a date where no protest occurred) the model predicted only twenty-six events that never happened.

To predict protest action on the basis of changes in the frequency of Google search terms is an impressive feat, but the pairing of this kind of "chatter" from media sources with event data has even broader-scale application – some of which remains veiled in secrecy. Recent years have seen an upsurge in using big data platforms and methodologies to create predictive models of political and social events. The U.S. Defense Advanced Research Projects Agency (DARPA), for instance, has an ongoing project called the Integrated Conflict Early Warning Systems (ICEWS), the aim of which is to predict social and political events. In keeping with DARPA's mission, the primary emphasis of ICEWS is on predicting inter- and intra-state conflict. Reportedly, the predictive models generated out of ICEWS have informed a number of important government actions, but at least parts of this data-gathering effort are available for public analysis.[11]

Looking at the application of ICEWS in conflict forecasting offers a useful example because of how machine learning is employed at two different stages of the forecasting process, in terms of gathering data and then leveraging it for forecasting. The basic premise of ICEWS is that it is a storehouse of millions upon millions of textual news stories, and this corpus of text is then the target of natural language processing algorithms that extract from these stories information about the event written about therein. Implemented on a vast scale, the data-collection efforts of ICEWS generate essentially a massive spreadsheet where every row is an event and the different columns of the spreadsheet contain data about the actors involved in an event, such as whether they are state or non-state actors as well as the nature of the interaction between the actors, including the degree of violence in the interaction.[12] The corpuses of text are truly massive, and their availability is only increasing over time with the advent of social media and the ability of other machine learning algorithms to recognize speech and convert it to text with a high degree of accuracy. The only way to even approach a comprehensive review of such a huge quantity of data is through computer-aided processing and coding, and fortunately with increasing advances in this field the automated process is at least roughly equivalent to the accuracy of human coders.

Once these data about events have been extracted from the text, using them for prediction is not very different in principle from the example using GT data above. One recent example is an analysis from Robert Blair and Nicholas Sambanis that aimed to forecast civil wars using ICEWS data.[13] In the early 2000s, Sambanis compiled a dataset (using human coders) that captured the occurrence of civil wars in states around the world. These data are at the country-month level, meaning that you can imagine a spreadsheet with a separate row for every country in every month of a year, across multiple years. For instance, there would be a row for the United States in January 2000, February 2000, March 2000, and so on, then another set of rows for Argentina in January 2000, February 2000, March 2000, and then finally rows for the United States in January 2001, February 2001, and the like. In the next column would be either a 0, 1, or a blank space, with a 0 indicating peace, a 1 indicating the initiation of a civil war in that month, and a blank space indicating ongoing civil war. The objective of relating the ICEWS data to the civil war data is thus to see whether changes in the rates or nature of events in these countries precede the appearance of a 1 in the civil war column in a consistent way.[14]

In their article, Blair and Sambanis used the ICEWS data to calculate counts of different events for countries in different months, aggregating up the number of events at the country-month level. This has the effect of adding additional columns to our spreadsheet, with an additional column for different types of events and the cell values indicating the number of that type of event in a country-year row. To give a stylized example, in a row for France in 2003 there might be three additional columns with values indicating the number of events where members of the public made demands of the government, the number of events of nonviolent political protest, and the number of instances of political violence. With the data set up in this format, estimating a forecasting model is a matter of downloading the appropriate software program, carefully setting up an already written function, and interpreting the results following standard practice in data science. In the case of Blair and Sambanis's analysis, this process yielded good results; the researchers were able to correctly predict in the overwhelming number of cases, with few false positives.[15]

IS THERE A FUTURE FOR PREDICTION?

Between developments in psychology that have identified best practices in extracting wisdom from the crowds, game-theoretic models that can predict the choices of elite decision-makers, and big data models that extract meaningful predictions from Internet chatter of everyday life, the forecast for forecasting is the best in human history. Does that mean, however, that the prospects are good? On that score, the response should be more equivocal, because forecasting techniques still have substantial weaknesses, and the path for integrating predictive analytics into governance is yet uncertain.

Returning to game theory, practitioners of this technique correctly assert that with sufficiently complex utility functions and powerful computing, strategic games can incorporate lying, deception, repeated interactions, bluffing, trust, and learning. Assuming adequate knowledge of the actors and the rules of a strategic interaction, criticisms of game theory as being reductionist are not particularly persuasive. On the other hand, there are some more unavoidable limitations. For one, game theory can fail when a strategic situation changes unexpectedly, as in cases of an act of God. Bueno de Mesquita describes one example of this in his own work, related to the Democratic Party's effort to pass health care reform during the first Clinton administration. He designed a strategic game for modeling the outcome of this effort and predicted it would be successful. What he failed to anticipate beforehand was that a prominent player in this process, Representative Dan Rostenkowski, would become embroiled in scandal in the middle of the reform effort, which changed the behavior of a key player and disrupted the outcome. Relatedly, game theory has very little to say about the probability of such events. Game theory can only model the behavior of strategic actors – that is, people or institutions. It has little or nothing to say about the likelihood of weather disasters, the rate of failure of jet engines, or the outlook for real estate prices in small cities in Appalachia.

One response to this might be that even if game theorists cannot predict the weather, a sufficiently robust statistical model drawing on previous weather patterns can. As the examples above show, advances in modeling and data collection are increasing the feasibility of predicting even rare events. But even there, limitations persist. Machine learning requires gathering a large amount of data about a system, identifying an outcome or classification of interest in that data, selecting a machine learning algorithm that will use that data to connect the predictors with the outcome, correctly interpreting those results, and then working to refine the data collection process and the implementation of the algorithm to improve prediction performance. While in a particular well-developed use case the application of machine learning can yield powerful sights, it also requires knowing what questions can be answered with the technology, what data need to be gathered, and the implementation of a development process for doing so. Here, machine learning software must begin to interface with human project management and workflows, the inefficiencies of which are the subject of untold numbers of MBA case studies and the object of scorn at many a faculty meeting.

Once human interactions are routinized and institutionalized, a bureaucracy has been born, and their record with respect to averting disaster is often quite poor. There are obvious circumstances in which the government has failed to anticipate or has ignored credible predictions of disaster in the past. To give just a handful of examples, consider the devastating damage to levees in New Orleans following Hurricane Katrina, the space shuttle *Challenger* disaster, the grounding of the 737 MAX airliner following several major accidents, and even the COVID-19 pandemic. In all these cases, reports after the fact led some observers to believe that decision-makers did not respond appropriately to the risks of disaster, with terrible economic and human costs. Indeed, there are several significant obstacles to the integration of prediction into bureaucratic and governmental processes, or at least to quickly making the transition to fully leveraging these techniques. Governmental bureaucracies produce huge quantities of data, but often these sources of data are siloed into proprietary systems and cordoned off for certain approved uses. With dozens of agencies collecting data in different formats and storing it in different formats and structures, it will take a massive effort for government enterprise to effectively share data across offices and agencies, and, as we will see more of, bureaucratic turf wars and tensions between agencies may make this process more difficult than need be.

A second issue that could limit the effective use of analytics and prediction in government is the tendency for bureaucracies to press on with preferred policy responses even in the face of countervailing evidence. We shall return to this topic in greater detail below, but it bears mentioning now as we explore prediction specifically. Even today, without adopting cutting-edge analytical methods to guide performance, it is well known that many federal programs are at best ineffective and at worst corrupt. Internal audits of government programs by Offices of Inspector General or the Government Accountability Office routinely indicate that the federal programs fail to meet critical goals, but very often the programs themselves persist despite such findings. Given this track history, there is serious reason to doubt how much bureaucracies would modify their behavior even if they knew the future. If a program is predicted to fail or a disaster is likely to arise from current policy with anything less than a degree of absolute certainty, it seems likely that the bureaucratic response would be to shrug and claim impotence.

The same reasoning extends to the political principals who are invested in the continued existence of bureaucracies. Politicians have short planning horizons and parochial goals. In the face of adverse prediction, a reasonable strategy could be to simply ignore a prediction, insulate against actual costs, and then obfuscate and blame others for the mess that follows. In other cases, politicians may actively root for the failure of certain programs or even for outright disasters, so long as it is not a disaster for them and is instrumental in their pursuit of other personal or professional objectives.

Another important obstacle to the integration of prediction and forecasting into government: there are some issues which simply cannot be predicted with any degree of certainty. In his recent book, legal scholar and sometimes behavioral economist Cass Sunstein analyzes the implications of such situations for efficiently crafting regulations.[16] Sunstein draws on the concept of "Knightian" uncertainty, which is a situation where multiple possible outcomes are readily imaginable but it is simply not feasible to estimate the probability of any given outcome occurring. Sunstein gives as an example a looming financial crisis. In a complex system like the financial system, there is always some baseline risk of a collapse, but it is essentially impossible to meaningfully estimate a probability that it will come in a given week, month, or year. There simply are not enough past crises in similar situations to form a basis for an expectation – it is not like a rolling weighted die several thousand times and then generating a probability distribution that can be the basis for future guesses about whether the die will show up with a 4, 5, or 6 on the next roll. In the face of such uncertainty, Sunstein proposes that government regulators should rely on what he calls the "maximin" principal – that is, taking whatever steps are necessary to avoid the most catastrophic of imaginable results.

Sunstein's recommendation is reasonable in settings where genuine catastrophe is a likely outcome, but there are some important additional implications. For one thing, to date the maximin principle has not been incorporated into regulatory thinking, which is what prompted Sunstein to write the book in the first place. Instituting a new decision rule in a bureaucratic system is a difficult endeavor, and so even if maximin is the appropriate response to Knightian uncertainty, implementing this across government when it is counter to existing practice is quite a heavy lift, given the resistance to change that is common in bureaucratic culture. A second issue associated with uncertainty, however, also poses a significant challenge. Often, even if an event is conceivable, the steps that would avoid that event are difficult to know. A classic example of this might be France constructing the Maginot line of fortifications on its eastern border with Germany after World War I. Designed to stop an anticipated German invasion, huge resources went into constructing a long line of fortifications. However, construction of the line ended at the Ardennes Forest, and of course the Wehrmacht simply drove through the Ardennes.

The Maginot line is a famous example of futility, but there are deeper concerns here. Social science struggles mightily to identify causes of social, economic, and political phenomenon. In qualitative settings, there are often too few comparable cases upon which to draw for purposes of confident inference, and in quantitative settings, many econometric techniques require powerful assumptions about the structure and properties of data for inference to be valid. The very concept of "statistical significance" that is at the heart of most social science inference is hotly debated, and there are significant questions about the policy relevance of many scientific results aimed at causal inference.[17] Even in what seems like the most obvious of circumstances, like the connection between smoking and lung cancer, it required decades for social scientists to convince the public of the robustness of their findings. Picking up an issue of the *New York Times* or reading other elite news sources, one can see that headline writers can misinterpret the results of scientific studies or overstate their certitude, in matters from nutrition to epidemiology to the dynamics of online dating. When many causal relationships are so difficult to tease out, designing policies meant to prevent unknowable outcomes is a difficult proposition.

Finally, we observe one more issue that makes us cautious about overselling predictive analytics going forward. If predictive analytics worked and spurred governments to take ongoing preventive action, then the disasters that they predict would, presumably, never happen at all. In such a case, the cost of major ongoing political and social action to prevent disasters will eventually be perceived as too great to prevent the disaster from happening. With short memories, the devastating costs of the event will fade, and the desire to prevent a non-routine disaster will seem less and less like a useful application of resources. It seems possible that we are seeing an example of this slippage in the slow crumbling of the Transatlantic Alliance and the neoliberal economic order. After the enormous trauma of World War II, the post-Bretton Woods international order was put into place with the intention of making such Great Power wars in Western Europe unthinkable. An entire security structure was developed and put into place to prevent it from happening again. So long as the USSR threat was in place, the value of this structure as a means to prevent interstate conflict seemed apparent. However, with that threat gone, the stable system that successfully prevented a potential event has similar shown cracks. President Trump was openly skeptical about the value of the Transatlantic Alliance throughout his administration, even going so far as commanding his subordinates to withdraw military forces entirely from Germany in the days following his defeat in the 2020 election.[18]

This pattern of memory loss – where successfully responding to a crisis makes the policy the victim of its own success – can also be seen in an example from U.S. domestic politics: the rolling back of the Voting Rights Act. Implemented in 1965, the Voting Rights Act included a "preclearance" provision which required certain states to seek approval from the Attorney General of the United States or from a panel of federal judges before enacting changes to election laws. The authorizing authority had to determine that the change would not have the purpose or effect of impacting the right to vote based on race or minority status. Shelby County, Alabama challenged the constitutionality of this procedure some 50 years later, arguing that it was an undue burden on the state that interfered with a state's right to control its election procedures.[19] Chief Justice John Roberts agreed, asserting that, "Nearly 50 years later, things have changed dramatically,"[20] and as such, the factors in favor of the protective measures no longer withstood constitutional scrutiny. No doubt Roberts was correct that minority representation and participation is far healthier than in the Deep South in 1964, but his assumptions about what would happen once the preclearance provision ended were arguably wrong. In the wake of President Trump's reckless and undemocratic attacks on the integrity of voting systems in the 2020 election, many states began implementing new restrictions on voting rights that would have, at a minimum, been subject to significant scrutiny in the pre-*Shelby* courts. Indeed, it is difficult to maintain vigilance once it seems a battle has been won.

A Gloomy Forecast?

What we have said here should not entirely dissuade governments from adopting cutting-edge analytic technologies to the maximum extent possible. There are certainly many cases where forecasting can save the government money and improve the quality and responsiveness of government services. These include applications like preventing Medicare fraud, planning maintenance for public infrastructure, and other tools that streamline the delivery of government services. We do not intend to gainsay the value of these kinds of applications, which save billions of dollars and may enhance the quality of government services and the public's confidence in them. In situations where data are easy to gather, problems easy to define, and solutions to those problems do not threaten prized programs, there is plenty of opportunity to improve the quality of government with the application of analytics.

If put in the broader context of the ongoing discussion between truth and power in our society though, we cannot help but feel a bit underwhelmed by these applications. Governments are certainly interested in filling potholes or identifying at-risk youth. However, history is defined not by such quotidian government tasks. The oracular visions of Delphi that have come through the ages are not about the rate at which Hector should have been replacing the axles of the chariots at a more frequent pace. What generations past sought to learn at Delphi was when Thera was going to erupt, when the Mongol *orda* was coming over the horizon, or whether the rains would come in Tenochtitlan. On that front, we are less sanguine about prospects of prediction. Developments in predictive technologies seem on the edge of providing good insights into the future, even for comparatively rare events like civil wars or pandemics – the kind of black swan events that have become the subject of so much discussion in recent decades. However, the political trade-offs required to reshape anticipatorily significant kinds of human action are extremely challenging for a large, diverse democratic society, filled with divergent and entrenched interests.

We also cannot forget that the application of analytics in government risks not only incompetence, but indeed malevolence. It is increasingly apparent that the power of predictive analytics has a dark side. On one hand, there is an increasing appreciation of the problems of algorithmic bias. In tasks like automatic mortgage approvals, facial recognition, or recidivism rate calculations, AI applications have shown that they make systematic errors that negatively affect minority groups.[21] In another of the most common uses of predictive analytics, the algorithms that generate social media feeds have been the subject of great concern as a potential source for the distribution of extremist political media, and possibly as a wider driver of political polarization. Finally, in authoritarian systems, and most notably China, state-driven data-gathering and analytics has terrifying consequences for social engineering and the repression of minority groups.

Considering these patterns of slippage and the potential for misuse and inaccuracy, the policymakers who are interested in incorporating predictive analytics into governance will need to think hard about the appropriate strategy for doing so. It is a very tough task for politicians and the public to accept a restructuring of society based on a projection of some black swan in the future, especially if the costs of preventing such a disaster seem exceptionally high. However, a society that has social, economic, and political capital in the present will be better able to respond to catastrophic events as they happen, and credibly monitor and notify citizens when a disaster is coming.

Prediction may make for more efficient government and may help policymakers steer the state away from some icebergs. However, there will often be a gap between what is possible with analytics and the political systems' ability to prepare and plan for such unknown outcomes. Cassandras will still cry out, and the government will not always hear – at least not to the satisfaction of the disgruntled residents of Troy.

NOTES

1. Imbens, Guido W., and Donald B. Rubin. 2010. "Rubin causal model." In Steven Durlauf and Lawrence E. Blume, eds, *Microeconometrics*. London: Palgrave Macmillan, 229–242. https://doi.org/10.1057/9780230280816_28.
2. For a good introduction to modern econometric techniques for causal inference, see Angrist, Joshua, and Jorn-Steffen Pischke, 2009, *Mostly Harmless Econometrics*, Princeton: Princeton University Press.
3. Our organization of the literature is similar to Phil Schrodt's presentation at Indiana University in November 2020. Schrodt, Phil. 2020. "Technical Forecasting of Political Conflict." Presented at Indiana University, Workshop in Methods, Karl Schuessler Institute of Social Science, November 13. https://parusanalytics.com/eventdata/presentations.dir/Schrodt.Forecasting.IUB.pdf.
4. Kahneman, Daniel. 2011. *Thinking, Fast and Slow*. New York: Farrar, Straus, and Girous.
5. Tetlock, Philip E. 2005. *Expert Political Judgment: How Good Is It? How Can We Know?* Princeton: Princeton University Press.
6. Tetlock, Philip E., and Dan Gardner. 2015. *Superforecasting: The Art and Science of Prediction*. New York: Crown.
7. For another assessment of prediction as a form of expertise, covering some common material, see Nichols, Tom, 2017, *The Death of Expertise*, Oxford: Oxford University Press.
8. One could also begin with Von Neumann, but Nash is especially relevant today.

9. Bueno de Mesquita, Bruce. 2009. *The Predictioneer's Game: Using the Logic of Brazen Self-Interest to See and Shape the Future*. New York: Random House.
10. Timoneda, Joan C., and Erik Wibbels. 2021. "Spikes and Variance: Using Google Trends to Detect and Forecast Protests." *Political Analysis* (April). https://doi.org/10.1017/pan.2021.7.
11. O'Brien, Sean P. 2010. "Crisis Early Warning and Decision Support: Contemporary Approaches and Thoughts on Further Research." *International Studies Review* 12(1): 87–104. https://doi.org/10.1111/j.1468-2486.2009.00914.x.
12. ICEWS data and documentation is available at https://dataverse.harvard.edu/dataverse/icews.
13. Blair, Robert A., and Nicholas Sambanis. 2020. "Forecasting Civil Wars: Theory and Structure in an Age of 'Big Data' and Machine Learning." *Journal of Conflict Resolution* 64(10): 1885–1915. DOI: 10.1177/0022002720918923.
14. The missing rows would be dropped from the analysis because the model is not designed to predict the end of civil wars, only their initiation. In that sense, an ongoing civil war is useless data in this context; the interest is when the column switches from a 0 to 1 only.
15. This summary slightly oversimplifies the results, because Blair and Sambanis compared the performance of several competing modeling strategies, but these numbers are representative of the overall results.
16. Sunstein, Cass. 2021. *Avoiding Catastrophe: Decision Theory for COVID-19, Climate Change, and Potential Disasters of All Kinds*. New York: NYU Press.
17. For an excellent overview of the policy relevance of much of social science research, see Imbens, Guido, 2021, "Statistical Significance, p-Values, and the Reporting of Uncertainty," *Journal of Economic Perspectives* 35(3): 157–174. DOI: 10.1257/jep.35.3.157.
18. Swan, Jonathan, and Zachary Basu. 2021. "Episode 9: Trump's War with His Generals." *Axios* May 16. www.axios.com/off-the-rails-trump-military-withdraw-afghanistan-5717012a-d55d-4819-a79f-805d5eb3c6e2.html.
19. *Shelby County v. Holder*, 570 U.S. 529 (2013).
20. Id.
21. Lee, Nicole Turner, Paul Resnick, and Genie Barton. 2019. "Algorithmic Bias Detection and Mitigation: Best Practices and Policies to Reduce Consumer Harms." Brookings May 22. www.brookings.edu/research/algorithmic-bias-detection-and-mitigation-best-practices-and-policies-to-reduce-consumer-harms/.

3. Crisis and decision-making

In the last chapter, we explored the ongoing dialogue between experts and decision-makers by focusing on the matter of prediction – that is, the ability of experts to meaningfully guide the exercise of power by forecasting what was to come. We suggested that although the technology of prediction continues to improve, the prospects for meaningfully incorporating those insights into governance were not as bright as some might hope. Experts, however, are not limited to *ex ante* support of political and bureaucratic leaders. Experts are also present during crises, and their role in how tumultuous events unfold deserves analysis as well.

In his chapter on the Melian Conference, Thucydides in *The History of the Peloponnesian War* describes how the Melians failed to listen to the expertise of their Athenian opponents, instead relying on an appeal to gods. As Thucydides said, war is a harsh teacher, and the Melians quickly fell.[1] What Thucydides said of war might also be applied to other sorts of existential crises, including economic collapse, environmental disaster, and plague. Those who fail to think logically court disaster. Jared Diamond, for example, identifies several cases, including the collapse of the ancient Mayan civilization, in which political decision-makers failed to respond to looming environmental crises, with disastrous results.[2]

But crisis not only punishes those who fail to learn; it also rewards attentive students. Those able to think rationally, adapt, plan, and listen to realistic advice can survive and prosper. In Tokugawa Japan, for example, decision-makers confronted with environmental crises endeavored to learn how to deal with them. In the 17th century, the shogunate employed forestry experts to solve the nation's near-disastrous woodlands crisis involving the severe depletion of the nation's forests. The result was that Japanese silviculture prospered to the benefit of the nation.[3] Or, to return to martial examples, both the United States and the Soviet Union learned from their initial World War II military blunders and recovered to defeat their antagonists.

Crises, to be sure, can produce enormous stress for a society and its decision-makers. Take, for example, the incredibly tense moments during the 1962 Cuban Missile Crisis, when President John F. Kennedy and his advisers faced the prospect of nuclear war with the Soviet Union.

> Defense Secretary Robert McNamara: Mr. President, there are a number of unknowns in this situation I want to comment upon, and, in relation to them, I would

like to outline very briefly some possible military alternatives and ask General Taylor to expand upon them.

But before commenting on either the unknowns or outlining some military alternatives, there are two propositions I would suggest that we ought to accept as, uh, foundations for our further thinking. My first is that if we are to conduct an air strike against these installations, or against any part of Cuba, we must agree now that we will schedule that prior to the time these missile sites become operational. I'm not prepared to say when that will be, but I think it is extremely important that our talk and our discussion be founded on this premise: that any air strike will be planned to take place prior to the time they become operational. Because, if they become operational before the air strike, I do not believe we can state we can knock them out before they can be launched; and if they're launched there is almost certain to be, uh, chaos in part of the east coast or the area, uh, in a radius of six hundred to a thousand miles from Cuba.

Uh, secondly, I, I would submit the proposition that any air strike must be directed not solely against the missile sites, but against the missile sites plus the airfields plus the aircraft which may not be on the airfields but hidden by that time plus all potential nuclear storage sites. Now, this is a fairly extensive air strike. It is not just a strike against the missile sites; and there would be associated with it potential casualties of Cubans, not of U.S. citizens, but potential casualties of Cubans in, at least in the hundreds, more likely in the low thousands, say two or three thousand. It seems to me these two propositions, uh, should underlie our, our discussion.[4]

Fortunately, with war imminent, the Soviets withdrew their missiles and none of the possibilities mentioned by McNamara came to pass.

A full reading of the transcript of this meeting reveals an incredible level of tension in the room. The president and his advisers understood that the decisions they made or did not make could lead to the deaths of millions of Americans "uh, in an area in a radius of six hundred to a thousand miles from Cuba." Would there be a general nuclear war? What communications did the Soviets have with their forces in Cuba? Might the Cubans, themselves, launch an air attack against nearby American cities? During the meeting, as the president and his chief advisers considered these matters, their focus was total, and their attention to even small military details sharp. They showed little interest in matters not germane to the immediate military situation and waved off efforts by some in the room to introduce normally but not immediately important political and diplomatic considerations.

We often think that high levels of stress and anxiety undermine careful planning and rational thought, and sometimes they do. However, stress can also have the effect of improving learning, memory, performance, and attention to detail. Indeed, some studies have found that under conditions of high stress, concentration is enhanced and interference from less relevant information filtered out, as seemed to be the case in the meeting discussed above.[5] This effect is prompted by the stress-induced release of cortisol and offers a definite evolutionary advantage. An animal faced by a crisis, say an encounter with a predator, is more likely to survive if it can muster a burst of energy and focus even if, over the long term, high levels of stress may be damaging. In the short term, however, individuals can even learn to make conscious use of stress to help them accomplish tasks and solve problems.[6] Many veteran public performers, including academic speakers, know that pre-performance "jitters" and anxiety are necessary for a good performance. Experienced performers use their anxiety to provide the energy needed to hold the rapt attention of the audience.

Individuals faced with risk or crisis-induced stress tend to narrow the focus of their attention and think more carefully about their actions.[7] They are more willing than at other times to learn, to consider new ideas and perspectives, and to modify their behavior.[8] They also seek advice. Experimental evidence suggests that individuals are more likely to solicit and accept advice when the stakes are high.[9] As in the missile crisis example above, it is during periods of stress and crisis that individuals are most likely to turn to advisers and exhibit a willingness to follow suggestions they hope will help them resolve pressing concerns. Unfortunately, however, some of the shortcomings of expert advice can arise in times of crisis.

GETTING GOOD ADVICE

President Kennedy, like other government and corporate executives, employed professional advisers. In Kennedy's case, military officers, intelligence experts, political operatives, and a score of others were available to offer expert opinions on the course of action most likely to eliminate the threatening Soviet missiles and avert nuclear war. The president received excellent advice from most of these experts and within two weeks compelled the Soviets to remove the missiles without having to fire a single shot.

As we have noted, Americans have always been ambivalent in their feelings about experts. On the one hand, America is proud of its scientific and technical expertise. American universities and think tanks employ tens of thousands of experts whose advice is sought by decision-makers and frequently broadcast and quoted by the mass media. Tens of thousands of economic, intelligence, military and other subject-matter experts are employed by the federal government and tens of thousands more are employed by state and local governments. On the other hand, America's Jacksonian heritage has left a certain residue of contempt for experts. The "mad scientist" is a stock literary character, and Peter Sellers's infamous Dr. Strangelove was a fictitious national security adviser whose expert advice was about facilitating the destruction of humanity. Even American experts on the matter of expertise caution readers to be skeptical of experts' claims.[10]

Even so, expert advice, particularly on scientific and technical matters, is invaluable. More than two thousand years ago, Socrates observed that in debates in Athens's Assembly, topics such as building or ship construction were taken to be the business of builders and shipwrights, and anyone who, though no expert, attempted to give advice in those areas was jeered off the platform. Similarly, the Roman philosopher Cicero declared that the cultivation of and reliance upon technical experts had provided the Romans with "healthcare, navigation, agriculture ... exports or imports ... quarrying of iron, copper, gold and silver ... houses ... aqueducts, canals, irrigation works, breakwaters and harbours."[11]

Today, only rather foolish individuals – and, unfortunately, there are quite a few – reject the healthcare recommendations offered by physicians or the legal advice proffered by attorneys in favor of something they may have read on the Internet or heard from a neighbor. And for their part, national decision-makers usually benefit from listening to experts, particularly in times of crisis. Take the matter of public health. For the most part, despite early fumbles, the U.S. national government eventually received sound and well-tested advice from its epidemiological experts in the face of the 2020 COVID-19 pandemic. Many of the principles adduced by these experts, including sanitation, isolation, restrictions on movement, surveillance, quarantine, contact tracking, and so forth, were based upon long-tested principles that can be traced back to policies developed by Italian city states to address the plague in the 15th century. Indeed, the first permanent board of health experts, the Sanita of Venice, was established in 1486, also in response to the plague.[12]

A century ago, during the 1918 influenza pandemic, public health experts recommended that schools be closed and large public gatherings cancelled. Where local decision-makers refused to heed this advice, the results were disastrous. In September 1918, the mayor of Philadelphia, in the face of expert advice, refused to cancel a "Liberty Loan" parade designed to show enthusiasm and raise money for the war effort. The result was that thousands of individuals attending the parade became infected and, as the disease spread through the city, it produced more than twelve thousand deaths.[13] Philadelphia's public health experts were correct, but the city's obdurate leaders would not listen and made a disastrous decision. One cannot help but see parallels to this in the COVID-19 pandemic, as when popular Fox News commentator Tucker Carlson routinely denounced unelected experts and attacked their authority to guide federal policy.

If the recognized experts were always correct, life would be simple. Faced with a problem, decision-makers would need only to turn to the best-qualified domain experts for advice and the appropriate course of action would be followed. Unfortunately, however, recognized medical, economic, military, and other experts are sometimes wrong. And they can be wrong at the worst of times – in the face of crises caused by unique events (black swans) – when accepted, tried and true responses are inadequate or even irrelevant. In such crises, recognized domain experts sometimes fall victim to cognitive entrenchment and refuse to accept the possibility that they are dealing with a novel situation requiring new modes of thought. Communities of established experts, moreover, are over time likely to converge around some accepted set of beliefs that will be defended by the entire community against contrary claims made by interlopers and even against contrary evidence.[14] In turn, the failures of established experts may then open the way for new perspectives. Let us consider several such cases and see what they might have in common.

The Great Depression: From Liquidationism to Keynesianism

At the outset of the Great Depression, as stock prices fell, the banking system neared collapse, major firms closed their doors, and unemployment rose sharply, U.S. President Herbert Hoover turned for advice to the nation's foremost economic experts, led by Secretary of the Treasury Andrew Mellon. These experts, who included many of the leading economists of the day, advised Hoover to take no action at all. Most subscribed to a set of ideas that came to be known as "liquidationism."[15] In the liquidationist model, economic depressions were an unfortunate but unavoidable element of economic growth, needed to "liquidate" failed investments and force the redeployment of capital from unprofitable to more profitable uses. Accordingly, the government did not seek to use fiscal or monetary policy to bolster demand and stimulate the economy.

Eminent Harvard economist Seymour Harris declared that the Federal Reserve should not endeavor to bolster the banking system but should, instead, view bank failures as necessary to promote future expansion.[16] For his part, Joseph Schumpeter, one of the preeminent economists of the period, wrote that economic depressions should not be seen as evil, but were essential to create the conditions for progress. Attempting to shelter banks, businesses, and other investments from the effects of a depression would merely ensure that capital would continue to be employed in unproductive ways. Indeed, Schumpeter argued, government efforts to stimulate business activity would prevent the proper liquidation of unproductive assets and produce a worse depression later. In his memoirs, President Hoover complained bitterly about the advice he had been given:

> The 'leave-it-alone liquidationists' headed by Secretary of the Treasury Mellon ... felt that government must keep its hands off and let the slump liquidate itself. Mr. Mellon had only one formula: 'Liquidate labor, liquidate stocks, liquidate the farmers, liquidate real estate' ... He held that even panic was not altogether a bad

thing. He said: 'It will purge the rottenness out of the system. High costs of living and high living will come down. People will work harder, live a more moral life. Values will be adjusted, and enterprising people will pick up the wrecks from less competent people.'[17]

The economic ideas underlying liquidationist thought were by no means absurd. In fact, the liquidationist model applied very well in some historical situations such as the expansion of the American rail system in the 19th century, with which mainstream economists were familiar.[18] The problem, however, was that the model became so entrenched in economic thought that orthodox economists sought to apply it to all situations and, moreover, members of the economics community in good standing tended to regard it as gospel.[19] Whatever its intellectual virtues, liquidationism could not be applied to as severe, sustained, and widespread an economic calamity as the Great Depression in which all capital, productive along with unproductive, was at risk. In this time of economic crisis, advice from recognized experts was off the mark.

Franklin D. Roosevelt, who took office in 1933, had no particular understanding of economic theory beyond the idea that balanced budgets were a good thing, and his closest advisers, members of the "Brain Trust," consisted almost entirely of lawyers and included only a single professional economist. One of the administration's first major economic programs, the National Industrial Recovery Act (NIRA), was a poorly conceived effort to raise prices by reducing production that, if anything, resulted in higher levels of unemployment. Neither Roosevelt nor his advisers, however, were strongly committed to any particular economic theories, and they soon came under the influence of a set of ideas associated with John Maynard Keynes.

Keynes had become an influential economist in Britain during World War I. After the war, however, he fell into disfavor with the government and the economics profession more generally because of his advocacy of then unpopular causes. Keynes was highly critical of the Versailles Treaty which compelled Germany to pay substantial reparations – a policy popular with Germany's victorious foes. In his 1919 book *The Economic Consequences of the Peace*, Keynes argued, prophetically, that these reparations would impoverish Germany and could lead to dangerous political and social instability.[20] In the 1920s, Keynes was among the few to advocate the depreciation of sterling to make British exports more affordable, and opposed British participation in the international gold standard, which would have a deflationary effect on the economy at a time of high unemployment. Keynes came to be regarded as an outsider and his ideas had little influence.[21]

The crisis of the Great Depression and the inability of leading economic theorists to offer viable solutions created an opportunity for such an outsider to influence policy. Keynes did not anticipate the 1929 stock market crash and lost nearly all his assets. The ensuing economic collapse stimulated Keynes's thinking and in 1933 he published *The Means to Prosperity*.[22] Addressed to the British and American governments, this volume made specific policy recommendations. In general terms, Keynes advocated abandoning the idea of balanced budgets and non-interference with the business cycle. He proposed sharply increasing government spending and incurring deficits to bolster employment, consumer demand, and growth. The book was widely read and began to influence academic as well as popular discussions of economic policy. In 1936, Keynes presented his full theory in his *General Theory of Employment, Interest and Money*, one of the most influential economic treatises of the past century.[23] Keynes admitted that his policy prescription might have some deleterious effects in the long term, but he declared that it would have the immediate-term effect of increasing employment and ameliorating the effects of the Depression. Most importantly, Keynes provided a blueprint and rationale for government action rather than passivity in the face of a crisis. He said that traditional economists

> believed that the existing economic system is in the long run self-adjusting, though with creaks and groans and jerks, and interrupted by time lags, outside interferences and mistakes. Those [like himself] on the other side of the gulf, however, rejected the idea that the existing economic system is, in any significant sense, self-adjusting.[24]

By the late 1930s, Keynes's views had become fully accepted by official Washington. As Herbert Stein observes, Keynesianism suited the needs of the Roosevelt administration because it provided a formula that offered an immediate way out of the Depression – deficit spending to bolster employment and increase aggregate demand. Keynesianism also legitimated something else sought by the New Dealers but opposed by their conservative foes, namely the construction of a large and powerful national government able to correct the putative failures of the private sector.[25] Keynesianism became more than an economic theory. It was, for Americans, a new social outlook in which the state bore responsibility and exercised power to correct the shortcomings of civil society.

What should we learn from this history? To begin with, the inability of established domain experts to offer advice that would ameliorate the ravages of the Great Depression offered an opening for individuals with new ideas. Many ideas were, in fact, put forward by persons without any claim to economic expertise. Minnesota's Farmer-Labor governor, Floyd Olson, presented a vision of a "cooperative commonwealth" in which all key industries would be taken over by the government. Louisiana governor Huey Long proposed a "share our wealth" program in which all personal fortunes would be confiscated and the proceeds used to give every American family enough money to acquire a home, a car, and a radio. Radio priest Father Charles Coughlin preached that the monetization of silver would bring an end to the Depression, which he blamed on the nation's worship of the "pagan god of gold." Charles Townsend led a movement that convinced millions of Americans that prosperity could be restored if the government would provide a pension of $200 a month to every citizen over 60 on the condition that he or she retire and promise to spend the money within one month. When critics pointed out that Townsend's financial estimates made no sense, Townsend declared his indifference to mere numbers.[26]

Unlike Long, Townsend, and the others, Keynes was a well-trained economist, an undoubted domain expert who happened to hold views different from those professed by the leading figures in his field. Keynes certainly possessed credentials and experience similar to those of the leading economic experts of the day. What he lacked was cognitive entrenchment that prevented him from dismissing accepted ideas and developing alternative advice for decision-makers. It is also notable that Keynes appears to share many of the qualities of a perpetual beta, the personality orientation described by Philip Tetlock and introduced in the previous chapter. These are individuals who are open-minded and constantly seeking to analyze, adjust, and improve rather than settle upon some fixed perspective. Keynes had originally been trained in mathematics rather than economics. He was interested in classics and philosophy and drew upon a variety of perspectives when addressing economic problems.[27] He wrote on probability theory and was an active journalist and revised his theories in light of experience. As we shall see, Keynes seems to typify the sort of expertise needed in a time of crisis.

War: The Harsh Teacher

Cognitive entrenchment is by no means exclusively a civilian phenomenon. Military commanders seem quite prone to this shortcoming. It is sometimes said that officers who rise to the top in peacetime armies possess political and bureaucratic rather than martial skills. In the Soviet army of the 1930s, for example, officers were promoted on the basis of political reliability while thousands of able and experienced officers were purged for some real or imagined disloyalty to the regime.[28] Command of most units was usually shared between a military officer and a political cadre who might have no military expertise.

For their parts, the top commanders of the army, generals Timoshenko, Voroshilov, and Budenny, were old civil war cronies of Soviet leader Joseph Stalin. Stalin initially depended upon these long-established and loyal experts for military guidance but as their military advice, based upon experience in an earlier era of warfare, proved useless, Stalin turned to a new generation of officers, including Marshal Georgi Zhukov, to lead the army. Stalin never fully trusted Zhukov, whom he always suspected of plotting against his own leadership. However, with the survival of the Soviet state in serious doubt, Stalin saw that he had no choice. As Thucydides would have understood, Stalin had to learn or perish.

The Soviet Union's military problems stemmed from the fact that politics had trumped military expertise in the appointment of officers. Even the best of professional armies, however, may have difficulty coping with unanticipated threats and crises. And, very often, the problem is cognitive entrenchment on the part of even the most able and experienced military experts. Take the case of the Israeli army in 1973, when one of the world's premier military forces was nearly defeated by a blow for which it should have been prepared. On October 6, 1973, the Egyptian and Syrian armies launched coordinated attacks against Israeli forces on the Golan Heights and Suez Canal. In both arenas, Israeli defensive positions were lightly manned. Israel depended upon early warning and rapid mobilization to deal with security threats. In this instance, however, the Israelis had failed to anticipate the severity of the threat and suffered grievously as a result.

Equipped with sophisticated anti-tank and anti-aircraft weapons, as well as cutting-edge night vision equipment, more than 30,000 Egyptian troops of the Egyptian Third Army and other forces crossed the Suez Canal and breached the Israeli fortifications on the other side. At the same time, Egyptian anti-aircraft missiles held the vaunted Israeli air force at bay. By October 9, the Israelis had blunted the Egyptian advance, though at a cost of heavy losses in troops and equipment. An Israeli counterattack across the canal trapped the Egyptian Third Army, but a U.S.-brokered ceasefire ended the fighting with the Egyptians in possession of a swath of territory they had captured on the east side of the canal. In the Golan Heights, a Syrian force of 28,000 troops, 800 tanks, and 600 artillery pieces attacked an Israeli force numbering only some 3,000 troops supported by fewer than 200 tanks. The Syrian attacks were well executed and they very nearly retook the Golan Heights, which had been captured by Israel in the 1967 war. Israeli reserves were rushed to the Golan and in two weeks of heavy fighting were able to drive the Syrians back. As on the Suez front, Israeli casualties were heavy.

Israel's near defeat at the hands of the Egyptians and Syrians has to be understood primarily, as Cohen and Gooch observe, as a failure to anticipate their enemies' intentions.[29] The Israeli military consists of a small standing force backed by an army of well-trained reservists who can be mobilized and deployed if the situation requires it. Because such a mobilization disrupts the civilian economy, threat assessment is a well-developed art in Israel. In October 1973, however, the threat was not properly assessed and reserve forces were not mobilized in a timely manner.

The problem was not lack of information regarding Egyptian and Syrian troop movements. Israel possessed an excellent intelligence service. Through various forms of surveillance Israeli intelligence carefully monitored Egyptian and Syrian troop movements. Intelligence sources in the Arab world warned that a heavy attack was imminent. In the days preceding the war, the Soviet Union evacuated diplomatic personnel and military dependents from Egypt and Syria, signaling Soviet knowledge that hostilities were imminent. Possession of key pieces of information, however, did not persuade Israeli intelligence experts that an attack was imminent. Senior Israeli intelligence experts, particularly the well-respected head of Israeli intelligence General Eliyahu Zeira, were wedded to a particular concept that made them blind to their opponents' intentions. Zeira and his senior officers were confident that Egypt lacked the ability to mount a serious challenge to the Israeli military and so would refrain from undertaking a major offensive.[30] These same experts thought that Israel would easily deal with anything short of an all-out attack. Senior intelligence experts also failed to understand the importance of Egyptian and Syrian improvements in weapons, training, and doctrine since the 1967 Arab–Israeli war. In short, leaders of one of the best intelligence services in the world suffered from a cognitive entrenchment that left their nation in grave peril.

This same sort of cognitive entrenchment helps to explain the Japanese defeat at the Battle of Midway in June 1942, the turning point in the Pacific War. The Japanese naval commander, Admiral Yamamoto, who had led the devastating attack against the Americans at Pearl Harbor, was convinced that the American fleet had been thoroughly demoralized by the Pearl Harbor disaster and subsequent defeats in the Pacific. The admiral persuaded his superiors and the Japanese government to give him carte blanche authority to implement a strategy based upon these assumptions. Yamamoto believed that the task before him was to lure an unwilling and crippled foe into leaving its base in Hawaii and engaging the Japanese fleet in a decisive battle. This conviction led Yamamoto to scatter his forces in a manner designed to mask their true strength from a timid enemy rather than concentrate them in mutually supportive units to maximize their fighting power.[31]

Yamamoto was no fool and had been an innovative naval officer throughout his career, emphasizing naval aviation over surface combatants. During the 1930s, though he remained a popular star in the Navy, Yamamoto had infuriated Japanese militarists and the Imperial Army by questioning the invasion of China and the idea of an alliance with Germany against the United States. Like many Japanese naval officers, however, Yamamoto was a captive of the doctrines of American naval theorist Captain Alfred Thayer Mahan, who emphasized the nautical equivalent of the Napoleonic "decisive battle" to destroy the enemy fleet.

Yamamoto's assessment of the U.S. Navy was not without some foundation. The Americans had suffered defeats, and it had become clear that American equipment and tactical doctrine was, thus far, inferior to that of the Japanese. Hence, there might be reason to believe that the Americans would refuse to engage the full weight of the Japanese fleet. In its brief history as a modern naval force, moreover, the Imperial Japanese Navy had fought only foes reluctant to engage in battle. Both the Russian and Chinese navies had to be lured from their bases by a strategy of deception to be destroyed. This history reinforced Yamamoto's conviction that deception would be the best strategy.

So certain was Yamamoto of the assumptions underlying his strategy that he gave no credence to contrary evidence or to concerns raised by junior officers. The most important piece of information that might have discomfited Yamamoto was the result of the Battle of the Coral Sea fought between May 4 and 8, 1942, a month before the scheduled attack on Midway. At the Coral Sea engagement, American naval air forces went on the offensive, sinking one Japanese light aircraft carrier and severely damaging two Japanese fleet carriers. The U.S. fleet carrier *Lexington* was also sunk, but the Japanese plan to capture Port Moresby on New Guinea was foiled.

The U.S. Navy's aggressive action in the Coral Sea should have served as a warning to Yamamoto that his assessment of the Americans was not fully accurate. Instead, Yamamoto chose to interpret the result through the lens of his preconceptions. The battle was officially declared to have been a Japanese victory. True, an Imperial Navy light carrier, the *Shoho*, had been sunk. This loss, however, was attributed by Yamamoto and his senior officers to the shortcomings of that ship's officers and crew. The loss of a light carrier, moreover, was seen as a minor setback compared with the sinking of the *Lexington* and heavy damage inflicted upon a second American carrier, the *Yorktown*.

Whatever the losses they had sustained, the Americans had, in fact, been much more aggressive than anticipated and shown themselves to be capable of dealing severe blows to the Imperial Navy. These two facts flew in the face of the assumptions upon which the Japanese battle plan was based. Admiral Yamamoto, however, refused to allow the events of the Coral Sea to undermine his faith in his assumption that he must disperse his forces, hide his true strength, and lure the Americans to their destruction. This became very clear during war games conducted on Yamamoto's flagship as the Imperial fleet steamed towards Midway.

A junior officer playing the American side undertook a course of action that, as it later turned out, was very similar to the actual American battle plan. In the game, the Japanese carriers were heavily damaged, and the fleet forced to withdraw. Rather than accept this dangerous possibility, the young officer's superiors ruled his tactics out of bounds since, according to Admiral Yamamoto, the Americans were not possibly capable of undertaking such actions. The junior officer playing the role of the Americans was ordered to recast his move to be more consistent with Admiral Yamamoto's conception of what the U.S. Navy would do.[32] Later in the game, land-based bombers from Midway attacked and sank two Japanese aircraft carriers. The umpire ruled that only one had been sunk and even this one was later brought back to life. The war games persuaded many junior officers that Yamamoto's plan was severely flawed, but the admiral was not interested in criticism. Blinded by cognitive entrenchment, Yamamoto sailed blithely into a battle in which the Americans sank four irreplaceable Japanese fleet carriers and changed the course of the war.

Antidotes to Cognitive Entrenchment: The Perpetual Beta as a Crisis Manager

Established experts and decision-makers, as we have seen, can be guilty of cognitive entrenchment, not allowing any facts to undermine their confidence in assumptions which might have some validity but, under the circumstances, might lead to disaster. But what then? Though established economic experts in the 1930s seemed unable to formulate a plan to end the Depression, decision-makers certainly could not turn to Huey Long, Father Coughlin, Floyd Olson, or Charles Townsend for answers. Instead, in a time of crisis they were able to turn to theories advocated by an expert economist who had been out of favor with senior members of his profession and who, as a perpetual beta, lacked any entrenched commitments. Let us see examples of the "Keynes type" in the person of two other, seemingly dissimilar expert outsiders – Ulysses S. Grant and Winston Churchill.

Keynes had been born to an upper middle-class family and attended elite schools. Grant, for his part, was born into a poor family living in a country hamlet and received a modest education at home or in one-room country schools. Though seemingly untutored, Grant showed an interest in mathematics, literature, philosophy, and art. After securing a place at West Point through small-town political connections, Grant demonstrated considerable ability in mathematics and art and a keen capacity to draw accurate maps of places he visited.[33] Later in life, Grant became a voracious reader, devouring literary works to which he had not been exposed by his meager education. After his retirement, Grant wrote his memoirs while dying of cancer.[34] Indeed, he died only a few days after completing a final draft of the work in 1885. The *Memoirs* are one of the most important works of military history in the English language. They are clearly written, demonstrate an extraordinary understanding of military tactics, and include acute observations about the personalities of his friends and foes and the role of warfare in society. Mark Twain, albeit Grant's close friend, said,

> I had been comparing the memoirs with Caesar's Commentaries ... I was able to say in all sincerity, that the same high merits distinguished both books—clarity of statement, directness, simplicity, unpretentiousness, manifest truthfulness, fairness and justice toward friend and foe alike, soldierly candor and frankness, and soldierly avoidance of flowery speech. I placed the two books side by side upon the same high level, and I still think that they belonged there.[35]

Despite his intelligence, Grant's life prior to the Civil War included a series of failures. Not long after graduating from West Point, Grant found himself serving as a young lieutenant in the 1846–48 Mexican–American War. Grant thought the war was wrong – a campaign of conquest against a weaker nation designed to expand the immoral institution of slavery. Grant, nevertheless, served with distinction in the army, gaining considerable expertise in logistics, tactics, and the importance of taking an offensive stance. After the war, he was promoted to the rank of captain and assigned to a succession of bleak posts that seemed to have led him to drink excessively. In 1854 Grant was forced to resign from the army amid sometimes well-founded rumors of drunkenness that followed him for the remainder of his career. After his resignation, Grant engaged in a variety of unsuccessful business ventures, eventually spending unhappy days working in his family's leather goods shop in Galena, Illinois. Like his military career, Grant's civilian career seemed destined to end in failure.

Grant observed many years later that his unwelcome resignation from the U.S. Army proved providential. Had he remained in the army, he would have been a captain serving on some distant frontier post six years later when the war began. Instead, he was a civilian with badly needed military experience when the Northern states began to organize militia units.[36] As a result, Grant entered the war as a colonel commanding the 21st Illinois Volunteer Infantry Regiment. During a series of campaigns in the West, Grant defeated Confederate forces in several important battles that led President Abraham Lincoln to promote him, first from colonel to brigadier general and then to major general of volunteers. These promotions were opposed by many in the army hierarchy and by the Northern press after Grant's army sustained heavy casualties in the 1862 Battle of Shiloh. Lincoln rebuffed Grant's critics, reportedly saying, "I can't spare this man; he fights."[37] Grant's victories cleared Southern forces from the Mississippi River and effectively cut the Confederacy in half. In 1864, Lincoln promoted Grant to lieutenant general and gave him command of all Union armies.

During his campaigns in the West, Grant learned several important lessons that seem not to have been understood by the Union Army high command.

To be sure, many Union commanders, especially at the outset, were political appointees with no military credentials. Such generals as Benjamin Butler, Nathaniel Banks, John McClernand, and John C. Fremont were convinced of their own military genius and offered dangerous advice on the conduct of the war, in some cases sacrificing soldiers under their command on foolish missions that hindered the overall war effort. These officers were the military equivalents of Huey Long and Charles Townsend – ambitious but untutored individuals taking advantage of a crisis to attempt to make their marks.

But even those officers who, like Grant, were West Pointers who had fought in the Mexican–American War suffered from misconceptions about the war they were undertaking against the South. To begin with, some Union commanders, most notably including General George McClellan, who briefly served as general-in-chief of the Union Army, thought that the capture of Richmond was an important objective. The fall of the Confederate capital, they thought, would end the rebellion. The Northern press certainly supported this theory and made "Onward to Richmond" the nation's battle cry. Grant, however, believed that the destruction of the Confederate army, not capture of the Confederate capital, was the principal objective to be pursued. If the Confederate army was defeated, the capital would fall.[38]

Many Union generals, moreover, subscribed to what they called the "Napoleonic Idea," the idea that the Confederacy could be defeated in one decisive battle, demonstrating to the rebels that they must lay down their arms and return to the Union. This idea dominated Union strategy at the beginning of the war and helped pave the way for the North's defeat in the war's first major engagement, the First Battle of Manassas in 1861.[39] Later, General McClellan also favored the idea of defeating the South in one massive campaign in which he would overwhelm the Confederates with manpower and artillery. Grant, on the other hand, had seen for himself the futility of this idea. After his victory in the 1862 Battle of Shiloh, which had inflicted more casualties on the two sides than had ever been seen before in North America, Grant realized that the South was determined to fight and that the war would not be won with one battle. Grant later wrote, "Then, indeed, I gave up all idea of saving the Union except by complete conquest."[40]

Shiloh taught Grant that the Civil War would be a war of attrition in which the North would rely upon its superior numbers and superior ability to absorb casualties to erode the South's ability to continue the war. In the three-day Wilderness battle in 1864, Grant's army suffered 17,000 casualties and the Confederate army 11,000. In the subsequent Battle of Cold Harbor, the Union Army suffered more than 50,000 killed and wounded to the South's 30,000. The Northern press called Grant "the butcher" and demanded that Lincoln remove him from command. Grant, and by now Lincoln, understood that the Union could replace its losses while the South could not. It was by this terrible war of attrition and not by a single glorious victory that the South would be defeated.

A third article of faith among Union generals was that the war would be won in the East. It was, of course, in the East that the hundreds of thousands of soldiers of the Army of the Potomac and the Army of Northern Virginia faced one another and the largest battles of the war were fought. Grant, however, understood that the chief role of the Army of the Potomac in the East was to pin the bulk of the Confederate army's forces in place while Union armies struck from the West to destroy the Confederacy.

Finally, many Union generals seemed to focus on their own army's weaknesses and the enemy's strengths. McClellan, for example, was always convinced that his forces were outnumbered by Confederate forces that were in reality numerically inferior to his own. According to historian T. Harry Williams, McClellan "magnified every obstacle; in particular, the size of the enemy army increased in his mind the closer he got to it."[41] Grant had learned in his western campaigns that he should identify and strike at the enemy's weak points rather than become immobilized by dangers that might be lurking.[42]

After his appointment to command the Union Army, Grant communicated regularly with President Lincoln, with General Henry Halleck serving as an intermediary, to discuss his plans and reasoning. Lincoln, who had admired Grant from afar while the latter commanded armies in the West, saw that he now had a commanding general who was not wedded to various preconceptions about warfare but had, instead, learned from experience and adapted his tactics to fit circumstances rather than assume that circumstances would conform to his plans. If, through some magic of time and space, Grant rather than Yamamoto had commanded the Japanese fleet at Midway, the day might have gone differently for the Imperial Navy.

Like Keynes, Grant fit the description of Tetlock's perpetual beta discussed above – "trying, failing, adjusting, and trying again."[43] Grant had failed in civilian life and in the military, but he learned from his various failures. In the military realm, in particular, Grant learned small unit tactics, the critical importance of logistics, the superiority of the offense, the use of a staff system. Like a perpetual beta, Grant learned all these things through trial, error, experimentation, failure, and new effort. Lincoln observed that Grant was the first real general he ever had.[44] In a time of crisis, Grant was a general without the cognitive entrenchment of his fellow officers and so capable of fighting the war as it was, rather than the war they imagined.

If another example is needed of the beta as a crisis manager, we might look briefly at the career of Winston Churchill. Grant had been born to a poor family and Keynes to an upper middle-class family. Churchill was born to an aristocratic family that, on his father's side, was part of Britain's ruling elite. Churchill attended an elite boarding school but was an indifferent student.

After several failed attempts he won admission to the Royal Military Academy at Sandhurst and was commissioned as a second lieutenant in an elite regiment in 1895.

Churchill was first posted to India and participated in military campaigns in India and the Sudan, and he fought in the Boer War. He also became quite a well-known journalist. Churchill filed many dispatches from the various exotic outposts of the British Empire. These gained a readership at home, and his dispatches from South Africa were published as a volume which sold well.[45] Within a short period of time, Churchill became one of the United Kingdom's best-known military correspondents. He enjoyed the military life and enjoyed journalism but soon decided that his goal was to make himself a politician; indeed, a statesman.[46] Towards this end he resolved to make up the deficiencies in his education by reading widely in literature, philosophy, history, and science. After immersing himself in books for two years, Churchill believed that he was as well read as those of his contemporaries who had attended Oxford or Cambridge rather than Sandhurst.[47]

Returning to the United Kingdom in 1900, Churchill took a seat in the House of Commons and embarked upon his political career as a member of the Conservative Party. He soon made enemies in the Conservative leadership by opposing new tariffs, opposing an immigration restriction bill aimed at preventing new Jewish immigration, and supporting legislation aimed at protecting trade unions. Having lost favor with the Conservatives, Churchill stood for Parliament as a Liberal, and when the Liberals surprisingly won control of the government in 1906, Churchill was named to a junior ministerial position, Under-Secretary of State for the Colonies. In that role, he toured Africa and wrote widely read pieces for the British press.

So long as the Liberals remained in power, Churchill advanced steadily through the cabinet ranks, and in 1910 was appointed to the important position of Home Secretary, where he oversaw police and prison services. In a time when strikes and violent labor protests were common, Churchill was often clumsy, managing to anger both labor and management. In 1911, Churchill was named First Lord of the Admiralty, a position he held when World War I began. Churchill championed the disastrous 1915 Gallipoli campaign. This campaign was an unsuccessful effort to seize the Dardanelles, which produced nearly 200,000 casualties and very nearly brought down the government. Churchill was widely blamed for the campaign's failure and forced to resign his cabinet position and from Parliament. He returned to Parliament in 1917 and held positions in subsequent Liberal and, later, Conservative governments. Yet he was always tainted by the Gallipoli failure, and he did not recover the prestige or power he had lost in 1915. In the 1929 elections, the Conservatives were swept from power and though Churchill retained his own parliamentary seat, he was shunned, even by later Conservative governments. He would not hold a cabinet position again until 1939.

For a decade, Churchill served in Parliament but held no position of authority. Instead, he traveled, met with interesting people, read, and lectured, often speaking against Indian independence – a topic on which he eventually changed his mind. Churchill also wrote articles and books. Churchill's four-volume biography of his ancestor, John Churchill, the first Duke of Marlborough, was well received, as was his five-volume history of World War I. He published an autobiography which was briefly a best-seller. Above all, however, Churchill warned of the rise of German power and the need to oppose it.

With the benefit of hindsight, the United Kingdom's peril in the 1930s seems clear. Adolf Hitler, a brutal dictator at the head of a violent gang of thugs, had taken control of Germany. Within a short period of time, Hitler had rebuilt German industrial and military power and hardly bothered to hide his intent to subjugate his neighbors and dominate Europe. Yet, in the United Kingdom during the 1930s, elite opinion favored reaching some accommodation with Hitler. A common view within the British upper class, including the leadership of the ruling Conservative Party, was that a resurgent Germany represented a counterweight to the Soviet Union and that, all things considered, "Hitlerism was better than Communism."[48] This perspective led to a policy of appeasement towards Hitler. The British government avoided antagonizing the Germans, and it acceded to Hitler's various actions, including remilitarization of the Rhineland, annexation of Austria, and the partition of Czechoslovakia. Within the United Kingdom, the government instituted censorship to prevent the publication of news that might offend Germany or create an unfavorable climate of opinion towards the Nazis.[49] Speeches critical of Hitler by Labour or left-wing politicians were not reported by the mainstream press. Considering subsequent events, the term "appeasement" has become synonymous with a craven refusal to confront evil that is ultimately doomed to failure. In truth, however, appeasement is not necessarily a mistake and had always been an arrow in the quiver of British policymakers.[50] As Hans J. Morgenthau observed, appeasement is an appropriate policy instrument when dealing with a rival power generally satisfied with the status quo and merely seeking minor adjustments.[51] In such a case, appeasement and compromise can satisfy ambitions without disturbing the overall international order. Negotiation and appeasement became the norm in Europe during the period of the Peace of Westphalia ending the Thirty Years War. As Morgenthau goes on to observe, however, appeasement is doomed to failure in confrontations with an adversary harboring imperialistic ambitions. Such an adversary will never be satisfied with minor adjustments and will regard peace offerings as signs of weakness and a lack of resolve and will always demand more. Confronting imperialism with appeasement is always a recipe for disaster.

The problem, of course, is understanding an opponent's intentions. Hitler presented each of his territorial demands as the last demand he would make, couching his ambitions as necessary and proper adjustments in the status quo. Prime Minister Neville Chamberlain and the British leadership chose to believe him. Returning from Munich, Chamberlain claimed to have discerned Hitler's sincerity and thought himself to have achieved a great diplomatic success.

Anyone who had listened to Hitler's speeches, studied Nazi Party propaganda, and viewed German military preparations might have found reason to doubt that Hitler was merely seeking minor territorial adjustments. Hitler, indeed, had contempt for Chamberlain's foolishness. After the peace conference, Hitler remarked, "Our enemies are men below average, not men of action, not masters. They are little worms. I saw them at Munich."[52] Yet Chamberlain and much of the British establishment believed that they had done the right thing and averted war. Like Admiral Yamamoto, they sailed blithely forward, fitting the facts to their desired outcome.

Churchill, of course, took a different view of the negotiations with Hitler. Addressing the House of Commons on October 5, 1938, Churchill declared:

> We have suffered a total and unmitigated defeat ... you will find that in a period of time which may be measured by years, but may be measured by months, Czechoslovakia will be engulfed in the Nazi régime. We are in the presence of a disaster of the first magnitude ... we have sustained a defeat without a war, the consequences of which will travel far with us along our road ... we have passed an awful milestone in our history, when the whole equilibrium of Europe has been deranged, and that the terrible words have for the time being been pronounced against the Western democracies: 'Thou art weighed in the balance and found wanting'. And do not suppose that this is the end. This is only the beginning of the reckoning. This is only the first sip, the first foretaste of a bitter cup which will be proffered to us year by year unless by a supreme recovery of moral health and martial vigour, we arise again and take our stand for freedom as in the olden time.[53]

Why was Churchill able to discern what most other members of his social class and political party did not? Some possibilities suggest themselves. Churchill, like Keynes and Grant, was a domain expert who had been ignored. Though born into the nation's ruling elite, Churchill had been consigned to the political margins. He had been a failure; he had taken positions inconsistent with those of members of his class; his views had not been taken seriously for over a decade. As a result, Churchill had no personal or intellectual stake in the assumptions that drove the policies of Chamberlain and his fellows. Churchill was not cognitively entrenched, and they were. Churchill, moreover, was a model beta. He possessed a restless, inquisitive intelligence. He traveled, read, wrote, experimented, learned, failed, and tried again. Like his fellow betas, at the time of crisis Churchill could think clearly.

In Churchill's case, as well as those of Grant and Keynes, failure seems to have been an important factor. All three individuals had failed in the pursuit of conventional activities. Grant had been forced to leave the army and failed at business. Keynes lost his money in the stock market and his ideas were not accepted. Churchill was marked by his failure at Gallipoli and consigned to the political margins for a decade. Perhaps failure in conventional matters made all three open to thinking, as we might say, "outside the box," and imagining alternative possibilities not seen by their fellows.

Perpetual Betas and Decision-Making

Throughout the foregoing case studies, we saw glimpses of an interesting pattern. Tetlock's research on prediction, described above, suggested that individuals that operate in the so-called "perpetual beta" state have the greatest track record for making correct predictions. Comparing Yamamoto, Keynes, Grant, and Churchill suggests the possibility that such individuals are also best equipped to handle moments of crises. Rather than clinging to orthodoxy and continuing a plunge into disaster, the perpetual betas are willing to consider new theories and outlooks as they adaptively respond to the situations they face. Of course, we can only presume that figures like Keynes, Churchill, or Grant fall into this category. Unfortunately, they did not participate in Tetlock's Good Judgment Project, and while we infer their personality characteristics from the historical record, we cannot measure them directly.

As an alternative, we designed a short survey to measure the personalities and mindsets of members of the public and to relate those characteristics with responses to crises, both real and imagined. Using Amazon's Mechanical Turk service, we recruited more than 400 survey respondents and asked them several sets of questions related to how they would respond to crises, their views on expertise, and their trust in government and civil society. Afterwards, our participants completed several questionnaires drawn from social psychology and from Tetlock's work.

We used three different measures to tap into Tetlock's notion of a perpetual beta. First, we presented participants with a set of questions modeled on those that Tetlock used in his own work to distinguish the styles of reasoning of so-called "foxes" and "hedgehogs."[54] Second, we used a battery of questions that measured respondents' personalities using the five-factor model developed in the field of personality psychology.[55] In short, the "Big Five" model posits that individuals' personalities are reducible to five main components: conscientiousness, agreeableness, neuroticism (also called emotional instability), openness to experience (also called intellect or imagination), and extraversion. Tetlock noted that the style of reasoning of foxes was closely related to the openness-to-experience factor. Finally, we administered the twelve-item version of the intolerance of uncertainty scale (IUS), a measure developed by clinical psychologists that captures responses to uncertainty, ambiguous situations, and the future.[56] All of these measures are correlated with each other (p < .001) in the expected manner, with higher openness to experience being positively associated with "foxiness" (r = .31) and negatively correlated with intolerance of uncertainty (r = −.49), while intolerance of uncertainty is negatively associated with "foxiness" (r = −.21).

To assess the relationship between these measures and decisions in the face of crises, we presented respondents first with three hypothetical scenarios that reflected "crisis" situations. In one scenario, we put the respondents in the position of a sea captain in the 19th century. Under pressure to deliver a perishable cargo quickly, the respondents were told of reports indicating stormy seas ahead and asked whether they would be more likely to brave the storms or change to a course with a reasonable chance of avoiding storms but potentially taking longer. The second scenario presented the situation of a product manager concerned about the emergence of new competitors. Respondents had to decide whether to change their product to avoid being out-innovated. Finally, respondents were cast as lead singers in a rock band facing changes in musical taste; they had to decide whether to stick with their old tried-and-true act or take a risk and try out a new musical style.

To follow up on these stylized hypotheticals, we presented respondents with three real-world public policy dilemmas. We presented them with short statements about the ongoing risks of climate change, tax revenue shortfalls, and racial discrimination. In each case, respondents had to decide whether they preferred new actions in response to these problems or to continue with public policy as it currently stands.

For both the stylized hypotheticals and real-world policy dilemmas, we coded the responses so that a value of 1 indicated a preference of action and zero indicated support for the status quo. We then added up these values across all six questions, creating a score from zero to 6, and tested for relationships between these scores and respondents' scores on Tetlock's style-of-reasoning questionnaire, their scores on openness to experience in the Big Five, and their score on the intolerance-of-uncertainty scale. Using simple bivariate regression analysis, the figures below display the predicted scores on this six-point scale (on the y-axis) as a function of respondents' scores on each of the three personality measures (on the x-axis). The shaded areas around the lines are the 95 percent confidence intervals for the responses – an indication of the uncertainty about the range of possible responses at each x-axis value.

The pattern of results is unmistakable. Respondents with a foxlike style of reasoning and/or with higher scores for openness to experience were more prone to act in the face of current or impending danger than "hedgehogs" and those with low openness scores. Correspondingly, respondents that indicated a greater intolerance of uncertainty were less likely to act in the face of these dangers.

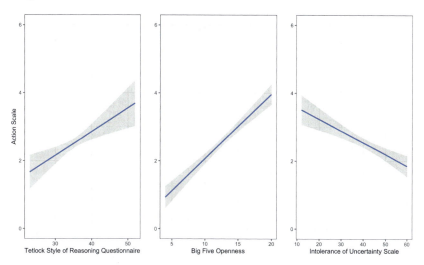

Figure 3.1   Personality traits and tendency towards action

Line is the predicated value based on an OLS regression model. Shaded area indicates 95% confidence interval

Experts in Crisis

A review of the case studies and survey data above presents a challenge for those looking to see expertise applied in elite decision-making settings. On one hand, much of professional education is focused on providing students with highly specialized sets of skills. Lawyers study law, engineers study engineering, and public managers are inculcated with standard texts and methodologies for organizational leadership. We see this tendency creeping into earlier stages of the educational process as well, as with the increasing emphasis on STEM (science, technology, engineering and math) and vocational training. As well, many educational settings avoid accountability for poor performance and are unwilling to saddle students with the awareness that they have made mistakes of judgment or failed to adequately prepare for challenges before them.

We see value in reducing the number of college graduates without employable technical skills, and we recognize that evaluation standards suffer from biases. But the case studies are indicative of the error of giving up on breadth and rigor in training and education. To summarize, Grant was a personal and professional failure until 1862, and in the next three years his strategy contributed significantly to the defeat of the most highly decorated graduate of West Point Military Academy, Robert E. Lee. Churchill may have come from an elite background, but he was a failed student and suffered public disgrace, only to return from his failures and correctly identify the threat of Nazism against prevailing conventional wisdom. Keynes, too, found himself professionally down and out, but in his exile he formulated the dominant approach to fiscal policy in the West for the next century. Had these individuals not been widely read and responded to their failures with intellectual curiosity, it stands to reason that they would not have had the insight and moxie to react creatively to subsequent crises. Perhaps a handful of case studies does not justify a hard and fast rule that the best leaders in crises are pulled from the professional dustbin, but these are three of the momentous crises of the 19th and 20th century. It seems worthwhile to at least shift our prior expectations about who exactly is most trustworthy when the chips are down and storms are gathering.

Our survey data suggests another intriguing takeaway about crisis and decision-making. Aside from preparing students in light of our models of successful leadership, it is not unreasonable to make potential leaders more aware of how their personality traits influence their decision-making processes. Our simple experiment provided evidence that pre-existing personality traits systematically affect decision-making processes, with individuals operating in perpetual beta mode being more likely than others to act in the face of crises. Additionally, personality traits were associated with the willingness to accept expert advice. These tendencies should be expected to be present in many decisional processes, but very little about our selection mechanisms in bureaucracies or politics is designed to account directly for such patterns. To the contrary, organizational incentives could be inadvertently leading to the promotion of hedgehogs into leadership positions who may be deep subject-matter experts but are temperamentally unsuited to respond to crises and incorporate expert insight into their actions.

If it is desirable for truth to speak to power, then it is likely desirable to put individuals in power that are best positioned to leverage it. The institutional reforms necessary to achieve this would be broad, from local school board curricula to civil service reform to electoral reform. Yet as technology advances and new tools are available to solve problems, the value of such tinkering only grows. Though it is counterintuitive, perhaps increasing the appreciation of failure and valuing personality over technical skill would be a wise direction in which to head. Absent that, stakeholders are likely to see more of their proverbial aircraft carriers sink needlessly to the bottom of the Pacific Ocean.

NOTES

1. For a broader discussion about war as an agent of rationality, see Ginsberg, Benjamin, 2014, *The Worth of War*, New York: Prometheus.
2. Diamond, Jared. 2011. *Collapse: How Societies Choose to Fail or Succeed*. New York: Penguin, 180.
3. Diamond 2011, 337.
4. Yale Law School, the Avalon Project. 2008. "Cuban Missile Crisis, Transcript of a Meeting at the White House, Oct. 16, 1962." https://avalon.law.yale.edu/20th_century/msc_cuba018.asp.
5. Chajut, Eran, and Daniel Algom. 2003. "Selective Attention Improves Under Stress: Implications for Theories of Social Cognition." *Journal of Personality and Social Psychology* 85(2): 231–248.
6. Rudland, Joy R., Clinton Golding, and Tim Wilkinson. 2020. "The Stress Paradox: How Stress Can Be Good for Learning." *Medical Education* 54(1): 40–45.
7. Taylor, Shelley E. 1991. "Asymmetrical Effects of Positive and Negative Events: The Mobilization-Minimization Hypothesis." *Psychological Bulletin* 110(1): 67–85.
8. Baumeister, Roy F., Ellen Bratslavsky, Catrin Finkenauer, and Kathleen D. Vohs. 2001. "Bad Is Stronger than Good." *Review of General Psychology* 5(4): 323–370.
9. Bonaccio, Silvia, and Reeshad S. Dalal. 2006. "Advice Taking and Decision-Making: An Integrative Literature Review, and Implications for the Organizational Sciences." *Organizational Behavior and Human Decision Processes* 101(2): 127–151.
10. Tetlock, Philip. 2017. *Expert Political Judgment: How Good Is it? How Can We Know?* Princeton: Princeton University Press.
11. Jones, Peter. 2017. "Socrates on Expertise: The Key is Knowing Their Limits." *The Spectator* February 11. www.spectator.co.uk/article/socrates-on-expertise.
12. Slack, Paul. 2012. *Plague: A Very Short Introduction*. New York: Oxford University Press.
13. Barry, John M. 2004. *The Great Influenza*. New York: Penguin.
14. O'Conner, Cailin, and James Owen Weatherall. 2019. *The Misinformation Age: How False Beliefs Spread*. New Haven: Yale University Press.
15. De Long, J. Bradford. 1990. *Liquidation Cycles: Old-Fashioned Real Business Cycle Theory and the Great Depression*. National Bureau of Economic Research Working Paper No. 3546. www.nber.org/papers/w3546.
16. Id. at 5.
17. Hoover, Herbert. 1952. *The Memoirs of Herbert Hoover*, Volume 3. New York: Macmillan and Co, 30.
18. DeLong 1990, 30.
19. See O'Conner and Weatherall 2019, ch. 4 for a discussion of expert conformity.
20. Keynes, John Maynard. [1919] 2013. *The Economic Consequences of the Peace*. New York: Olive Garden Books.
21. Skidelsky, Robert. 2005. *John Maynard Keynes, 1883–1946, Economist, Philosopher, Statesman*. New York: Penguin.
22. Keynes, John Maynard. [1933] 2006. *The Means to Prosperity*. London: Routledge.

23. Keynes, John Maynard. 1936. *The General Theory of Employment, Interest and Money*. New York: Harcourt, Brace and Co.
24. Quoted in Stein, Herbert. 1969. *The Fiscal Revolution in America*. Chicago: University of Chicago Press, 154.
25. Id. at 168.
26. Leuchtenburg, William E. 1963. *Franklin D. Roosevelt and the New Deal*. New York: Harper & Row, ch. 5.
27. Skidelsky 2005 at 43–46.
28. Glantz, David M. 2005. *Colossus Reborn: The Red Army at War, 1941–1943*. Lawrence: University Press of Kansas, 13.
29. Cohen, Eliot A., and John Gooch. 1990. *Military Misfortunes: The Anatomy of Failure in War*. New York: Free Press.
30. Id. at 126.
31. Parshall, Jonathan, and Anthony Tully. 2005. *Shattered Sword*. Washington, DC: Potomac Books.
32. Id. at 62.
33. Chernow, Ron. 2017. *Grant*. New York: Penguin.
34. Grant, Ulysses S. 2012. *The Complete Personal Memoirs of Ulysses S. Grant*. N.p.: CreateSpace Independent Publishing.
35. Twain, Mark. 1924. *Autobiography of Mark Twain, Vol. II*. New York: Harper and Brothers.
36. Chernow 2017 at 123.
37. White, Ronald C. 2016. *American Ulysses: A Life of Ulysses S. Grant*. New York: Random House.
38. Smith, Jean Edward. 2001. *Grant*. New York: Simon & Schuster.
39. Williams, T. Harry. 1952. *Lincoln & His Generals*. New York: Knopf.
40. Brands, H.W. 2012. *The Man Who Saved the Union: Ulysses S. Grant in War and Peace*. New York: Doubleday.
41. Williams 1952 at 27.
42. Smith 2001.
43. Tetlock, Philip E., and Dan Gardner. 2015. *Superforecasting: The Art and Science of Prediction*. New York: Crown, 190.
44. Williams 1952 at 305.
45. Gilbert, Martin. 1991. *Churchill: A Life*. London: Heinemann.
46. Roberts, Andrew. 2018. *Churchill: Walking with Destiny*. New York: Viking, 52.
47. Id. at 61.
48. BBC History. "Appeasement and the Road to War." www.bbc.co.uk/bitesize/topics/z7mxsbk.
49. Cockett, Richard. 1989. *Twilight of Truth: Chamberlain, Appeasement, and the Manipulation of the Press*. London: Palgrave Macmillan.
50. Kennedy, Paul M. 1976. "The Tradition of Appeasement in British Foreign Policy, 1865–1939." *British Journal of International Studies* 2(3): 195–215.
51. Morgenthau, Hans J. 1964. *Politics Among Nations*. New York: Knopf.
52. Perkins, Ivan. 2013. *Vanishing Coup*. Lanham: Rowan and Littlefield, 181.
53. National Churchill Museum. N.d. "Disaster of the First Magnitude, 1938." www.nationalchurchillmuseum.org/disaster-of-the-first-magnitude.html.
54. Tetlock 2017, ch. 3.
55. Donnellan, M. Brent, et al. 2006. "The Mini-IPIP Scales: Tiny-Yet-Effective Measures of the Big Five Factors of Personality. *Psychological Assessment* 18(2): 192–203. https://ipip.ori.org/MiniIPIPKey.htm contains the scoring key.

56. Measurement Instrument Database for Social Science. "Intolerance of Uncertainty Scale – Short Form (IUS-12)". Developed by Carleton, R.N., M.A. Norton, and G.J.G. Asmundson. www.midss.org/content/intolerance-uncertainty-scale-short-form-ius-12.

4. Speaking truth to bureaucracies

While politicians are not always known for modesty, at some level most know that they need help. Asked by citizens to help them resolve complex problems, elected leaders come to realize that running administrative bureaucracies that oversee government programs requires a level of specialization and expertise that is beyond their capacity or desire. Over time through this process, in the United States and around the world, legislatures have offloaded much of the day-to-day work of government to bureaucratic entities. There is a sound logic, in the abstract, to this transfer. Bureaucrats are in-house experts for the government, tasked with much of the details of policy formulation and administration. Government bureaucrats are also especially well positioned to interface with experts in academia, industry, and activist networks, and collectively these entities create policy systems that exert great control over the American economy.

But the transfer to authority is not without flaw, and bureaucracies have significant weaknesses as partners to experts and forums for the processing of expertise. As we will describe in this chapter, bureaucracies sometimes exhibit patterns of behavior that hamstring the policy process. As they persist and build their own institutional cultures, bureaucracies become jealous of their autonomy and prerogatives. Federal agencies become linked to a variety of political coalitions, and they use their political alliances to fight strongly to preserve their autonomy and prevent outsiders from intervening in what they see as their business. The agencies, for their part, may view the national interest through the lenses of their own interests, procedures, and agendas rather than from some neutral and objective perspective.[1] This sets up an ongoing competition between political and bureaucratic leaders as they vie for control over the administrative state.

The implications of this for the dialogue between truth and power are readily apparent. Political and bureaucratic leaders have preferred experts, and the administrative state becomes an extension of the conflicts between them. Indeed, those who seek to offer advice or direction to bureaucracies are likely soon to discover that agencies march to their own drummers and are most likely to accept advice with which they agree while ignoring expert opinion that is inconsistent with the agencies' own predispositions. We can see the consequences of this easily in the early stages of the COVID-19 pandemic when, for example, according to many media reports, the Centers for Disease Control (CDC) ignored external experts and insisted on using a flawed testing metric that for several critical weeks made test results all but uninterpretable.[2] And, as the epidemic spread, the CDC continued to ignore external experts and joined President Trump in downplaying the danger.[3] Either way, by ignoring established experts or later bending to political forces, the CDC failed to serve the public interest. Later, apparently protecting its own bureaucratic turf, the CDC refused to share data with other government agencies relevant to the question of whether booster shots might be needed to mitigate the threat of new COVID variants.[4]

In short, we argue that while bureaucracies are theoretically created as a mechanism for infusing governmental action with expert insight, it is wise to temper such expectations. As we will see, bureaucracies have the power to strategically filter expert advice, and while they resist it, they can be co-opted for political purposes.

THE FEDERAL ADVISORY COMMITTEE ACT

Data collected under the terms of a little-known but important piece of federal legislation, the Federal Advisory Commission Act (FACA), offer a remarkable window into the extent to which government agencies are interested in listening to the views of expert outsiders. Enacted in 1972, FACA sets out rules under which agencies organize advisory committees (FACs) staffed by experts from outside their own ranks to review agency activities and offer documented, albeit generally non-binding, advice to agency executives.

The way the federal agencies treat this potentially useful resource offers an enlightening commentary on the difficulties of speaking truth to bureaucratic power. FACA formalized a long-standing but otherwise unregulated practice of the Executive Branch, turning to outside commissions, committees, and other groups for advice and insight into policymaking.[5] FACA created procedures and criteria for the creation and maintenance of advisory committees, as well as reporting requirements. Today, data on advisory committees are collected and made available to the public by the General Services Administration (FACA Database).[6] Though small relative to the magnitude of the federal government, FACs have grown to be an objectively massive undertaking. In 2017, there were at least 7,500 meetings of FACs – an average of twenty a day. Since their inception, FACs have made tens of thousands of recommendations to the federal government. FACs cost the government more than $300 million per year. In 2017, there were more than 35,000 FAC members. Members include a huge range of individuals, from research scientists to bankers to representatives from local business, consumer, or conservation groups.

Given the magnitude of this enterprise, FACA committees have been the object of controversy over the years. Although they have not become law, Congress has shown an interest in reforming the FAC process. Representative

William Lacy Clay introduced legislation in the 110th, 111th, 112th, and 114th Congress to increase public access to FACs, clarify ethics requirements around them, and extend FACA requirements to certain committees formed by federal contractors.[7] Senators Rob Portman and Maggie Hassan joined these efforts with the FACA Amendments Act in 2019.[8] These efforts were widely supported among government transparency advocates, and they mirrored recommendations made by organizations like the Administrative Conference of the United States and Union of Concerned Scientists.[9]

The more dramatic actions with respect to FACA committees have come from the Executive Branch. In 1993, as part of its government reform efforts, the Clinton administration ordered the termination of one-third of all FACs other than those created by Congress, required agencies to justify the existence of those that remained, and banned the creation of new FACs unless "compelling considerations" existed. In 1994, Clinton extended this effort by requiring executive departments to create planning and review processes for new FACs. Subsequent administrations have engaged in similar "reform" activities. The Trump administration set a drastic limit of 350 FACs.[10] As with Clinton though, there was a caveat, and OMB could continue to authorize waivers for committees beyond the limit.

Trump's actions towards advisory committees were especially controversial at the Environmental Protection Agency (EPA). The EPA was a ripe target for such an order, as only one-third of its committees are required statutorily, with the rest created under the discretionary authority of the agency or the president.[11] With this flexibility, the Trump administration sought to eliminate many of the EPA committees, and it also moved to replace some special government employees, who are typically viewed as independent experts in committee deliberations.[12] One approach to changing committee composition was the requirement that no researcher receiving funding from the EPA could sit on an advisory board, a move that effectively barred many academics who, while subject-matter experts, relied on the agency for their research dollars.[13] Critics assailed these moves, characterizing them as anti-science, and the Government Accountability Office later found that some of the moves were improper.[14] In 2021, the Biden administration dismissed more than 40 advisory panel members who had been appointed by the Trump administration from EPA committees. According to one former EPA official, none of the deposed Trump-appointed advisers was unqualified to serve, but "the mix of people did not adequately represent mainstream science" – at least as viewed from the perspective of the agency.[15]

Though they attracted perhaps the most attention at EPA, the Trump administration's efforts were not isolated to that agency. In the Department of Interior, the administration did not need to force changes on advisory committees; the entire membership of at least one committee simply resigned in protest over disagreements with Secretary Ryan Zinke's leadership.[16] Also in Interior, the Trump administration prioritized the discontinuation of the Invasive Species Advisory Committee, which had a long history of clashing with agricultural interests at the Department of Agriculture.[17] At the Department of Commerce, it comes as no surprise that one of the committees prioritized for elimination was the Smart Grid Advisory Committee, which explored policy options that were not in the interest of conventional power plants and fuel suppliers.[18] Another of the FACs eliminated at Commerce was the Marine Protected Areas Committee, which was responsible for providing expert advice on conservation issues.[19]

It is interesting to compare the Trump administration's actions at EPA, Interior, and Commerce regarding FACs that favorably aligned with Democratic priorities with how the Biden administration treated Department of Defense (DoD) committees in its first few months in office. Just as the Trump administration declared bureaucratic war on disfavored agencies and FACs, the Biden administration followed the same pattern with DoD – which, as we shall see below, is typically viewed as a reservoir of Republican bureaucratic strength. In the waning days of the Trump administration, Acting Secretary of Defense Chris Miller installed Corey Lewandowski and David Bossie – two notorious figures in the Trump administration orbit without any national defense experience – into positions with the Defense Business Board.[20] This is best interpreted as a method of "burrowing" Trump into the federal government, perpetuating the influence of the administration even when out of office while "rewarding" loyalists and supporters. Predictably, the response of the Biden administration was swift. Within a month of the inauguration, new Secretary of Defense Lloyd Austin purged every member of DoD advisory boards over which he had discretionary authority to appoint or remove.[21] Austin took this opportunity to order a "zero-based review" of all FACs, requiring DoD officials to "conduct an in-depth business case of every sponsored advisory committee, supported by fact-based evidence for continued utilization of the advisory committee."[22]

The examples of the EPA and DoD ably demonstrate how political motivations can overtake a bureaucratic architecture that, in principle, is designed to emphasize technical expertise and support rational policymaking. However, even here, the reality is that bureaucracies have the ability to persist in the face of such pressure. As mentioned above, even as the Trump, Clinton, and Biden administrations took steps to curb FACs or root out disfavored members, each administration expressly included "escape hatches" that could potentially be used to save preferred committees. Committees could be spared if they could muster a compelling argument for their existence to OMB or the Secretary – forums where "compelling" has no legal definition and falls under the discretionary judgment of the administration. Indeed, conducting such a review is no guarantee that a bureaucracy can be eliminated. In 2020, a year after the Trump administration ordered massive cuts to FACs, the Department of Energy had eliminated only two advisory panels, and both of those were inactive to begin with.[23] Unsurprisingly, this was a relief to outside interest groups like the Union of Concerned Scientists and Energy Sciences Coalition, who had continued to advocate for the existence of the committees even after the blanket order for cuts had been issued. As one leader of the Energy Sciences Coalition stated, Department of Energy leadership had made a strong case to the administration to allow them to continue with their FACs, and as such the agency was essentially left alone to its own devices. To the contrary, in fact, in the time since the original Trump order, Secretary of Energy Rick Perry *reconstituted* at least one influential advisory board, and Congress *mandated* the launch of a new one, the National Quantum Initiative Advisory Committee.[24] There can hardly be a clearer example than this of a bureaucracy's ability to persist and even thrive in the face of political pressure, so long as it is at least not directly working against a political principal's interests.

This review indicates that FACs are a useful example of how political and bureaucratic conflicts seep into the process of evidence-based policy development, but despite this, FACs have received relatively little scholarly attention. What scholarship does exist confirms the takeaway from the evidence already presented: although allegedly a source of technical expertise, the creation, staffing, and use of FACs reflect well-worn patterns of bureaucratic and political conflict. In a focused study of the National Drinking Water Advisory Council (an EPA FAC), Balla and Wright found that interest groups can use public endorsements to influence agency appointments of FAC members.[25] They further concluded that Congress designs FACs and their membership requirements to ensure that preferred policy voices have access to regulatory decision-making. Again, this finding accords with the review completed above. In his analysis of FACA, Brown investigated the application of the principle of "balanced" membership in FACs, which is embedded in FACA and requires committees to include representation of a fair range of viewpoints.[26] Brown finds that a "double standard" characterizes the application of the balance principle, with agencies selecting expert members in terms of their professional qualifications but representative members in terms of political interests. This is problematic, Brown argues, because experts and representatives have both technical and political interests; evaluating each in terms of only one of these is therefore unrealistic.

Two more recent studies have investigated the composition of advisory committees, focusing especially on their ideological composition. Feinstein and Hemel combined data on FAC members with data on government officials' campaign contributions, and their analysis showed that FAC appointees in Democratic administrations tend to lean left, and those in Republican administrations tend to lean right.[27] They also find that agencies tend to create committees when the preferences of civil servants and the presidential administration are incongruent. An analysis by Miller, Curry, and Kennedy points to a similar conclusion, finding that political polarization characterized the staff of a single advisory committee in the Department of Justice.[28]

These findings are helpful in underscoring how FAC membership is ideologically driven, but the FACA data are rich, and provide other important insights into how bureaucracies collect and apply outside opinions and expertise. While the ideological composition of members is an interesting feature of FACs, it is only one dimension the characteristics of committees. FAC members can also be characterized on the basis of the kind of input they provide to committees. "Representative members" are selected to represent the point of view of groups outside the federal government, including industry, labor, or consumer organizations. By contrast, "special government employees" are intended to be outside experts who exercise independent judgment, based on expertise.[29]

Examining FACs in terms of the composition of their members as experts and interest group representatives provides additional insight into how the committees serve political and bureaucratic interests, perhaps more so than the interests of collecting "pure" expertise. A few questions are of interest. First, do agencies differ in their propensity to operate FACs? Second, how does the composition of FACs in terms of proportion of experts and outside representatives vary across agencies? Third, do agencies differ in their likelihood of adhering to the recommendations of FACs?

Our analysis here is confined to 25 Cabinet-level and other large agencies, covering fiscal year 2019. To begin, there are apparent differences in the propensities of agencies to utilize advisory committees. Figure 4.1 displays the overall number of FAC committees in that year.[30] As the figure indicates, FACA implementation differs substantially across the federal government, with some agencies making very little use of such committees and others drawing on thousands of outside experts.[31]

This high degree of variation is also apparent from Figure 4.2. Here, the y-axis value of each point is the percentage of representative-type members that make up advisory committees in that agency. As the figure ably demonstrates, there is tremendous variation in the character of these FACs, beyond the political ideology of any particular member. For some agencies, FACs are primarily home to outside interest groups, while in a smaller number the FACs are home to members identified for professional subject-matter expertise.

Aside from staffing patterns in FACs, there is no consistent pattern of committees generating recommendations for agencies or of agencies listening to the advice of FACs. Agencies track the number of recommendations each committee generates, as well as the proportion of a committee's recommendations that are implemented by an agency. Figure 4.3 shows the number of

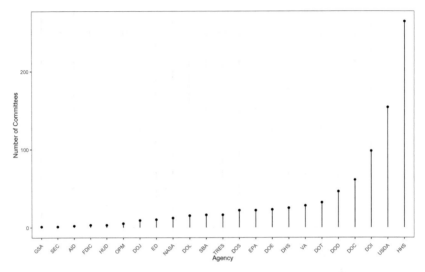

Figure 4.1   Number of FACA committees by agency, FY 2019

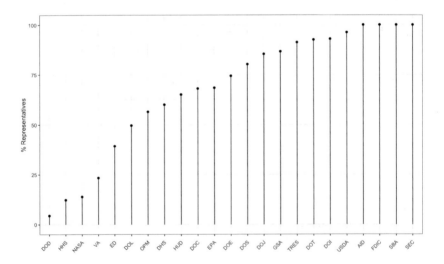

Figure 4.2   Proportion of representative FACA members by agency, FY 2019

Values on y-axis indicate proportion of FAC members in an agency that are designated as "representatives"

recommendations generated by the committee from the date of inception up to 2019 across 24 of the 25 selected agencies.[32] Beyond the wide variation in the productivity of FACs in terms of producing recommendations, agencies are also quite uneven in terms of the rate of adoption of FACs' recommendations. Figure 4.4 displays the percentage of FAC recommendations that were fully implemented between 2005 and 2019. While some agencies report high imple-

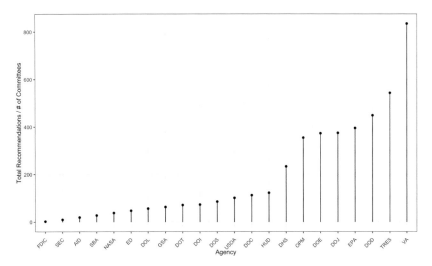

Figure 4.3   *FACA recommendations per committee by agency, FY 2019*

Values on y-axis indicate the total recommendations presented divided by the number of FACs within the agency

mentation rates, others appear to pay little heed to the FACs they convene.

These data tell a story about the ability of agencies to collect and leverage "expertise" to support their activities, in the context of broader bureaucratic and political forces. While partially serving as a forum for agencies to consult experts in the formulation of policy, in practice FACs also become forums for agencies to hear the voices of outside interest groups. Agencies use FACs inconsistently, and often not for the purposes of gathering "impartial" information. Further, while some agencies listen to the recommendations of their committees, others seem to barrel along with little heed to the advice they are given.

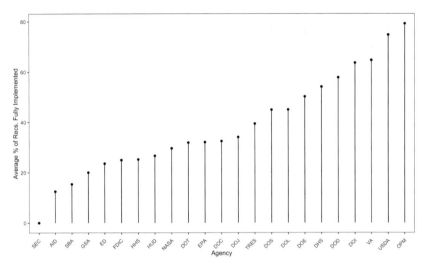

Figure 4.4   FACA recommendations implemented by agency, FY 2019

Values on y-axis indicate average proportion of recommendations fully implemented across committees

THE POLITICIZATION OF BUREAUCRATIC EXPERTISE

The FACA data are interesting because they show that agencies' actions are motivated by more than an innate desire to find and utilize the best possible advice in their decision-making process. The uneven implementation and adherence to FACA recommendations is a strong indicator of biased information search policies within the federal bureaucracy.

Imbalances and inconsistencies in federal advisory boards that few citizens have ever heard of might seem unimportant, but this must be viewed in the context of the larger role of bureaucracy and the growth of the administrative state in the United States. Today, many citizens take for granted the existence of a large federal bureaucracy. All Americans pay their taxes to the Internal Revenue Service, and most expect that the federal government will support them in their retirements with Social Security and Medicare. Americans also accept, perhaps begrudgingly, that the federal government has regulatory powers in areas like workplace and highway safety, as well as environmental matters. However, this has not always been the case. Until the Civil War, the federal government was very small, funded largely through customs duties. That conflict saw the temporary imposition of a federal income tax and an increase in federal authority, but Reconstruction saw the erosion of federal power, along with the protections of civil rights.

It was not until well into the 20th century that the federal government began to expand into the vast administrative state we see today. Roosevelt's New Deal saw the federal government engage in widespread financial regulation and the creation of a basic social safety net, along with the formation of the national security apparatus that is still with us today. In the post-World War II era, the public increasingly came to expect and accept that the federal government would have a stronger hand in solving policy problems. The key institutional innovation in this process was the growth in power of federal agencies vis-à-vis Congress.

Congress is largely composed of generalists whose skillset lies more in political rhetoric and organization than in detailed policy formulation. The demands on members' time and resources are extreme, divided between servicing their constituents, fundraising, and political campaigning. This leaves comparatively little time for policy formulation. The conundrum was solved by Congress over the course of the 20th century by delegating increasing amounts of power and discretion to the federal bureaucracy. The Administrative Procedure Act, passed into law in 1946, created the process by which policies are put into regulations via the rulemaking process. Through a series of judicial decisions capped off by the famous *Chevron* case, the courts sanctioned this transfer of policymaking power. As a result of these developments, today federal agencies have immense policymaking authority that is only loosely controlled by Congress. Agencies are stocked with specialists with deep expertise in both the bureaucratic processes of administrative policymaking and in the technical details of financial, environmental, occupational, agricultural, and many other domains of regulation. Certainly, Congress can still constrain agency action when it wishes through mechanisms likes the Congressional Review Act, but largely Congress no longer busies itself with the details of much regulatory policymaking.

As a result, while agencies operate under the nominal control of political principals in Congress and under different presidential administrations, in practice they have considerable independent authority. To complement their technical knowledge, agencies develop unique political cultures that are resistant to change, and they are known to resist "alien transplants" that might seek to control them.[33] The ability to fight with political principals and pursue their own independent ends has led to bureaucracies taking center stage at the heart of much larger political clashes.[34] One example is the battle over the Affordable Care Act (ACA), which occupied much of the Obama administration and the first two years of the Trump administration.[35] In one sense, the debate over Obamacare was about health policy and economics, but in another, it was a bureaucratic turf fight. The ACA had the effect of increasing the power of the federal administrative state. Though not to the extent of a single-payer health system, the Department of Health and Human Services acquired greater rulemaking authority through the implementation of the law – an agency that is widely considered to be progressive and an institutional ally of the Democratic Party. As such, the agitation of Republicans over the continued existence of Obamacare should be viewed in part as frustration over how the ACA enhanced bureaucratic authority.

The conflict over the ACA was in large part focused in Congress, and was about the institutionalization of greater administrative power in the hands of an agency seen as favorable to Democrats. At other times, bureaucratic conflicts take place more directly within the Executive Branch. It has become common for presidents to become engaged in serious conflict with their own bureaucracies, which serve as proxy wars in political fights. It is not only that presidents do not have perfect control over the bureaucracy and frequently struggle to use it to implement their preferred policies; beyond that, bureaucrats have the ability to damage the political fortunes of a president through what that scholars of bureaucracy call "shirking and sabotage."[36] Shirking and sabotage can occur at even the most mundane level of slow-walking policy implementation, but the impeachment of Donald Trump is a more dramatic example.[37] In his first impeachment, Trump was caught asking the Ukrainian government to dig up "dirt" on the business dealings of Hunter Biden, the son of his political rival Joe Biden.[38] Trump was exposed by a series of career bureaucrats who became aware of his maneuvers and provided this information to Congress. Trump railed over the loyalty of his administration, and to an extent he correctly diagnosed the problem – the administration's bureaucrats did indeed sabotage Trump's "policy." As Trump's administration continued, he seemed to become more aware of the need to control the bureaucracy through his appointees, using "acting" agency heads to bypass the congressional confirmation process and generally working to degrade the performance of disfavored agencies like the EPA or the Consumer Financial Protection Bureau (CFPB).

Other examples of bureaucratic conflict in the Trump administration stemmed from the COVID-19 pandemic. In April 2020, just a few months before his defeat in the 2020 presidential election, President Trump launched an offensive against federal regulatory agencies.[39] To hasten the reopening of the economy in the wake of business closures forced by the COVID-19 pandemic, the White House sought to suspend or repeal many federal regulations affecting businesses. The president and his advisers believed that the economic and public health crisis gave them a new opportunity to reduce the power of regulatory agencies controlled by their Democratic opponents. Democrats reacted with alarm to the administration's initiative, calling it "opportunistic," and pro-regulation interest groups attempted to thwart the administration's deregulatory effort.[40]

In a different vein, the Biden administration had its own struggles with the bureaucracy during the pandemic, in fact even involving FACA. In September

2021, a public fight developed between the CDC and the Food and Drug Administration (FDA) over the Biden administration's effort to encourage Americans to seek third-dose COVID "booster" shots. The CDC supported such boosters while the FDA opposed them. The FDA asserted that its review procedures had been short-circuited and its input ignored. As part of a "near mutiny" at the FDA, two high-ranking FDA officials turned in their resignations to protest this bureaucratic slight. Marion Gruber, Director of the FDA's Office of Vaccines Research & Review, and Deputy Director Phil Krause reportedly were furious that the CDC had intruded into a policy realm that they believed should be handled by the FDA.[41] Eventually, CDC Director Dr. Rochelle Walensky overruled the Advisory Committee on Immunization Practices – a FACA committee – and allowed the booster shots to move forward.[42]

Seen in this broader context, the implication of the FACA data should become clearer. FACs are an instance of agencies selectively and likely strategically formulating their diet of expertise. More importantly though, FACs are an example of the much broader entanglement between expertise and politics. On a conceptual level, federal agencies are occupied by neutrally competent bureaucrats that follow the directions of politicians and, directly thereby, the public. However, because of the processes of institutionalization and bureaucratization, expertise has increasingly become a weapon in political conflict. While a powerful tool, this comes with the consequences that the veneer of neutral competence is increasingly hard for experts to maintain. For expertise to be leveraged by federal agencies, it must be processed – some would say laundered – by agencies that are now well understood as combatants in partisan sieges.

One can imagine that being sullied by involvement in political competition would undermine the ability of experts to influence policy formulation. In fact, there is reason to believe this is happening, and now the administrative state may be at significant risk. In recent years, conservative justices on the U.S. Supreme Court have expressed skepticism about whether the power of the administrative state is consistent with the Framers' constitutional design.[43] These justices have expressed interest in reinvigorating an old legal principle formulated by the conservative Supreme Court of that era, which was opposed to Franklin D. Roosevelt's New Deal policies. In a series of cases, those justices argued that the Congress should be limited in its ability to transfer policymaking discretion to executive agencies by the "non-delegation doctrine." Following this rule, for a delegation of policymaking authority to be constitutional Congress cannot be overly broad or aspirational in its charge to agencies. Instead, the legislature must articulate an "intelligible principle" that guides the discretion of bureaucrats in the execution of policymaking authority. The Supreme Court stood down in a faceoff with FDR over an aggressive application of this rule, and for decades the Court has followed a liberal interpretation of the doctrine that allows for substantial agency authority. More recently, justices like Clarence Thomas and Neil Gorsuch have made statements suggesting they prefer a much more aggressive interpretation of the doctrine, requiring Congress to be far more specific about its expectations regarding how agencies would formulate regulatory policy. If this interpretation is applied forcefully, this could dramatically hamstring agencies in their efforts to implement any meaningful economic, environmental, or social regulation.

Jurists like Gorsuch, Thomas, Alito, and their kindred spirits in the Federalist Society may have some degree of intellectual dedication to the ideals of constitutional originalism. However, judges both liberal and conservative pair judicial philosophies with a set of political preferences, and frankly it stretches credulity to imagine that these reasoning processes operate in parallel, with no interference between the two. Given that, one is forced to wonder whether some of the animus towards agency authority embedded in the non-delegation doctrine is attributable to the increasingly political role that federal agencies have occupied over time. Even if the experts in these agencies are themselves scrupulously neutral, the organizations as a whole have become fortresses and actors in the political battles that we have described throughout this chapter. As one set of experts in the agencies has been co-opted into political conflicts, another set of experts in federal courthouses has taken the field in opposition. The melee is joined on all sides.

BUREAUCRACY AND POWER

Throughout this chapter, two important facts have emerged. One is that federal bureaucracies are fed and consume an uneven diet of expertise in their decision-making processes. Beyond that, however, agencies can no longer be viewed as impartial, neutrally competent bureaucracies. Even absent direction from political principals, agencies are likely to push forward with their own agendas, and they are nowadays frequently intertwined in political struggles, to the possible detriment of expert-driven policymaking.

Details about the management of the FACs may seem trivial, but bureaucratic conflicts are matters of serious political division. The efficient design of bureaucracy is an important element of the success or failure of a state. The military is a bureaucracy, as is the tax collection authority. The success of the Roman Empire could arguably be attributed to its skill in both these domains.[44] Similarly, the bureaucratic conservatism of imperial China was partially responsible for China's hesitance to continue the naval exploration of figures like the famed Admiral Zheng He.[45]

It may be a stretch to equate the recent bureaucratic politics in Washington, DC with world-historical patterns of rising and falling empires. However, it would similarly be wrong to marginalize the importance of the behaviors we have outlined in this chapter. Whether wisely or errantly conceived, federal bureaucracies wield immense power in the United States, with implications that are genuinely important for economic growth, human well-being, and, possibly, international competition. Bureaucracies are powerful but ungainly beasts. They are forged by a mixture of political and policy goals, and throughout their existence they serve as an arena for political competition and contention – with bureaucracies themselves self-animating and joining the fray. As the FACA data show, a consequence of this pattern of behavior is that "evidence-based" policies are not evenly or consistently applied throughout the bureaucracies, to the point that bureaucracies may not even listen to the advice they solicit. It might be difficult to imagine that the scrapping of Zheng He's fleet was a world-defining event, but in case it was, is it any less plausible to believe that a FACA committee's recommendation about climate change, the composition of the armed forces, or wide-reaching social policy could have similar unexpected but profound consequences?

NOTES

1. Bachner, Jennifer, and Benjamin Ginsberg. 2016. *What Washington Gets Wrong*. New York: Prometheus.
2. Willman, David. 2020. "How CDC Stumbled in Race for a Virus Test." *Washington Post* December 28.
3. Lewis, Michael. 2021. *The Premonition: A Pandemic Story*. New York: W.W. Norton.
4. Abutaleb, Yasmeen, and Lena H. Sun. 2021. "How CDC Data Problems Put the U.S. Behind on the Delta Variant." *Washington Post* August 19. www.washingtonpost.com/health/2021/08/18/cdc-data-delay-delta-variant/.
5. Stuessy, Meghan M. 2016. "Federal Advisory Committees: An Introduction and Overview." Congressional Research Service. R44253. https://crsreports.congress.gov/product/pdf/R/R44253.
6. Federal Advisory Committee Act Database. www.facadatabase.gov/FACA/FACAPublicPage.
7. Stuessy 2016.
8. Office of Senator Portman. 2019. "Portman, Hassan Introduce Bipartisan Legislation to Improve Transparency of Federal Advisory Committees." Press release April 11. www.portman.senate.gov/newsroom/press-releases/portman-hassan-introduce-bipartisan-legislation-improve-transparency.
9. Letter from Transparency Organizations. April 22, 2019. https://s3.amazonaws.com/demandprogress/letters/Letter_of_Support_for_the_Federal_Advisory_Committee_Act_Amendments_of_2019.pdf.
10. Katz, Eric. 2019. "Trump Orders Agencies to Slash Federal Advisory Panels." *Government Executive* June 19. www.govexec.com/management/2019/06/trump-orders-agencies-slash-federal-advisory-panels/157784/.

11. Farah, Nina, Kevin Bogardus, and Michael Doyle. 2019. "Trump Order Targets Advisory Committees." *E&E News* June 17. www.eenews.net/stories/1060612379.
12. Government Accountability Office. 2019. "EPA Advisory Committees." July 9. www.gao.gov/products/gao-19-280.
13. Bastasch, Michael. 2017. "Trump's EPA Will Get Rid of Science Advisers Who Get Taxpayer Funding." *Daily Caller* October 31. https://dailycaller.com/2019/02/13/dc-court-epa-advisory-boards/. Bastasch, Michael. 2019. "DC District Court Hands Trump's EPA a Major Victory over Environmentalists." *Daily Caller* February 13. https://dailycaller.com/2017/10/31/trumps-epa-will-get-rid-of-science-advisers-who-get-taxpayer-funding/.
14. Beitsch, Rebecca, and Miranda Green. 2019. "Trump's Order to Trim Science Advisory Panels Sparks Outrage." *The Hill* June 17. https://thehill.com/policy/energy-environment/448981-trumps-order-to-trim-science-advisory-panels-sparks-outrage. Tracy, Abigail. 2017. "E.P.A. Purges Scientists, Plans to Replace Them with Industry Reps." *Vanity Fair* May 8. www.vanityfair.com/news/2017/05/epa-scott-pruitt-scientists-dismissed. McCausland, Phil. 2019. "Trump's Order to Slash Number of Science Advisory Boards Blasted by Critics as 'Nonsensical'." *NBC News* June 15. www.nbcnews.com/politics/politics-news/trump-s-order-slash-number-science-advisory-boards-blasted-critics-n1017921.
15. Grandoni, Dino. 2021. "EPA Dismisses Dozens of Trump-Era Science Advisers Picked under Trump." *Washington Post* March 31. www.washingtonpost.com/climate-environment/2021/03/31/epa-advisory-panels/.
16. Beitsch and Green 2019.
17. Green, Miranda. 2019a. "White House Eliminates Advisory Boards for Marine Life, Invasive Species." *The Hill* October 1. https://thehill.com/policy/energy-environment/463893-white-house-eliminates-advisory-boards-overseeing-marine-life.
18. Green, Miranda. 2019b. "Trump Officials Eliminate Board That Advised on Smart Grid Innovation." *The Hill* October 9. https://thehill.com/policy/energy-environment/465001-trump-officials-eliminate-board-that-advised-on-smart-grid.
19. Green 2019a.
20. Kube, Courtney. 2020. "Defense Secretary Installs 2 Trump Loyalists to Pentagon Advisory Board." *NBC News* December 12. www.nbcnews.com/news/military/defense-secretary-installs-2-trump-loyalists-pentagon-advisory-board-n1250061. Edelman, Adam. 2021. "Trump Railed Against the 'Deep State,' but He also Built His Own. Biden Is Trying to Dismantle It." *NBC News* February 28. www.nbcnews.com/politics/politics-news/trump-railed-against-deep-state-he-also-built-his-own-n1258385.
21. Miller, Amanda. 2021. "Austin Slashes Hundreds of Volunteer Advisory Positions." *Air Force Magazine* March 9. www.airforcemag.com/austin-slashes-hundreds-of-volunteer-advisory-positions/.
22. Secretary of Defense. 2021. *DoD Advisory Committees – Zero Based Review*. https://media.defense.gov/2021/Feb/02/2002574747/-1/-1/0/DOD-ADVISORY-COMMITTEES-ZERO-BASED-REVIEW.PDF.
23. Clark, Lesley. 2020. "Trump Called for Killing Advisory Panels. What Happened?" *E&E News* June 22. www.eenews.net/stories/1063430131.
24. Id.

25. Balla, Steven J., and John R. Wright. 2001. "Interest Groups, Advisory Committees, and Congressional Control of the Bureaucracy." *American Journal of Political Science* 45(4): 799–812.
26. Brown, Mark B. 2008. "Fairly Balanced: The Politics of Representation on Government Advisory Committees." *Political Research Quarterly* 61(4): 547–560.
27. Feinstein, Brian D., and Daniel J. Hemel. 2020. "Outside Advisers inside Agencies." *Georgetown Law Journal* 108(5): 1139–1212.
28. Miller, Banks, Brett Curry, and Joshua B. Kennedy. 2020 "The Role of Advisory Committees in Bureaucratic Oversight: The Case of AGAC." *Congress & the Presidency* 48(2): 195–218.
29. Environmental Protection Agency. 2021. *Essential Guide for Members Serving on Federal Advisory Committees at EPA*. www.epa.gov/sites/default/files/2021-04/documents/2020_updated_faca_essentials_guide.pdf.
30. FACA data are reported by the fiscal year. Some individuals are members of FACs for multiple years. In this analysis, these members are counted multiple times, once for each year of FAC service.
31. The variation is similarly dramatic even when accounting for the differences in agency size.
32. The excluded agency is the Department of Health and Human Services (HHS), which is a massive outlier, with HHS committees generating more than two million recommendations, as compared with next highest number of recommendations of about twenty thousand in the DoD.
33. Seidman, Harold. 1998. *Politics, Position and Power: The Dynamics of Federal Organizations*, 5th ed., ch. 8. New York: Oxford University Press.
34. Ginsberg, Benjamin. 2022. *The Imperial Presidency and American Politics: Governance by Edicts and Coups*. New York: Routledge.
35. Lewis, David E., and Terry M. Moe. 2014. "The Presidency and the Bureaucracy: The Levers of Presidential Control." In Michael Nelson, ed., *The Presidency and the Bureaucracy*. Washington, DC: CQ Press, 374–405.
36. Brehm, John, and Scott Gates. 1997. *Working, Shirking, and Sabotage*. Ann Arbor: University of Michigan Press.
37. Ginsberg 2022.
38. Baker, Peter, Lara Jakes, Julian E. Barnes, Sharon LaFraniere, and Edward Wong. 2019. "Trump's Battle on 'Deep State' Turns on Him." *New York Times* October 23. www.nytimes.com/2019/10/23/us/politics/trump-deep-state-impeachment.html.
39. Burns, Katelyn. 2020. "The Trump Administration Wants to Use the Coronavirus Pandemic to Push for More Deregulation." *Vox* April 21. www.vox.com/policy-and-politics/2020/4/21/21229390/trump-administration-easing-regulations-coronavirus.
40. Whyte, Liz Essley. 2020. "Trump's Favorite Weapon in the Coronavirus Fight: Deregulation." Center for Public Integrity June 30. https://publicintegrity.org/politics/system-failure/trumps-favorite-weapon-in-the-coronavirus-fight-deregulation/.
41. Owermohle, Sarah. 2021. "Biden's Top-Down Booster Plan Sparks Anger at FDA." *Politico* August 31. www.politico.com/news/2021/08/31/biden-booster-plan-fda-508149.
42. Sun, Lena H., and Laurie McGinley. 2021. "Pfizer Booster Now Available to Older Americans and Those at Higher-Risk, Including on the Job, as CDC Chief

Partly Overrules Panel." *Washington Post* September 24. www.washingtonpost.com/health/2021/09/23/covid-booster-shots-cdc/.
43. For an overview of the conflict over the non-delegation doctrine, see Davis Mortensen, Julian, and Nicholas Bagley, 2020, "There's No Historical Justification for One of the Most Dangerous Ideas in American Law," *The Atlantic* May 26, www.theatlantic.com/ideas/archive/2020/05/nondelegation-doctrine-orliginalism/612013/.
44. See Gunther, Sven. 2019. "Politics of Taxation in the Roman Empire." Austaxpolicy Blog February 29. www.austaxpolicy.com/politics-taxation-roman-empire/. See also Gunther, Sven, 2016. "Taxation in the Greco-Roman World: The Roman Principate," In *Oxford Handbooks Online*. DOI: 10.1093/oxfordhb/9780199935390.013.38.
45. McNeill, William H. 1982. *The Pursuit of Power*. Chicago: University of Chicago Press, 44–45. See also Bachner, Jennifer, and Benjamin Ginsberg, 2016, *What Washington Gets Wrong*, New York: Prometheus Books, 204.

5. The truth is, using power is fraught with risk

Those wishing to speak truth to power, such as the advisers to the federal bureaucracy we introduced earlier, might do well to offer decision-makers an important but much-neglected bit of advice. The truth is that power is dangerous, and its use often leads to expensive failures and unanticipated and unwanted consequences. Power should be used cautiously and sparingly, and sometimes not at all. This is a reality that decision-makers seldom wish to hear. Those who command armies, bureaucracies, and police forces can easily come to believe that the power at their disposal will overcome every obstacle and allow them to achieve marvelous ends. This tendency is most closely associated with the American presidency, an institution that has been aggrandized out of all reasonable bounds over the course of the 20th and 21st centuries.[1] However, many in Congress and certainly many in the larger system of interest and lobbyist groups in Washington, DC, and in state capitols are loath to resist the temptation of political power. All politicians seek to be re-elected, increase their authority, achieve their policy goals, and prepare themselves for opportunities in their post-political lives. It is possible that some politicians can achieve these goals through inaction, but for the ambitious political leader the lure of action is strong.

Indeed, in contemporary America, while they may disagree on precisely what should be done, politicians, interest groups, and the media all seem to agree that power must and can be used to address the nation's problems. The idea of doing nothing seems off the table and is widely disparaged. Indeed, a congressional session that produces little highly publicized legislation is often ridiculed in the press as a "do nothing Congress." Nor is this tendency isolated to one party or the other. While Democrats seek an expansion of federal powers in response to issues like climate change or wealth inequality, the Trumpian mantra of "Making America Great Again" implies rolling back decades of economic, cultural, and political change, much of which is now deeply embedded in American society. Either way, the desire to wield political power to shift the status quo is firmly entrenched. Standing pat is a little-considered option.

There may be times when using governmental power is appropriate, perhaps in circumstances where thorny problems require coercion to resolve collective action problems or where only the government can pool and coordinate resources for projects of national importance. It may become necessary to use power, but the truth is – and this truth should be repeated loudly and often – that sometimes doing little or nothing is the best option under the circumstances. Acting even with the best of intentions exposes states and societies to new dangers that can leave them worse off than they were before. Among the most common dangers are planning failure, blowback and its close cousin thermostatic opinion, enforcement costs, moral hazards, rent-seeking, and the proliferation of fiscal evasions. At its most dramatic level, the application of "expertise" can lead to extreme moral outrages.

PLANNING FAILURE

The simple fact is that managing the provision of any service is a difficult task, rife with uncertainty. Car manufacturers produce models that do not sell, tech companies launch platforms and devices that gather no following, and media production studios put out box-office failures. The same holds true for government enterprises. Government programs can also fail because they are improperly scoped, under-resourced, or badly conceived from the start.

Many programs exemplify what Flyvbjerg and Sunstein call "the planning fallacy." This is a belief, to which many executives cling, that their knowledge and planning abilities will produce successful outcomes. In fact, for a myriad of reasons planners seem unable to predict, around the world many if not most programs fail.[2] Curiously, if perhaps not surprisingly, frequent failure does not seem to discourage governments from trying. However often they fail, politicians and executives often believe that action is the answer, and failure merely a temporary setback. The unofficial motto seems to be even if you never succeed, try, try again. In this way, social services and defense contracts are renewed year after year, while every administration suggests that its new management techniques will help the government run more like a business.

The continuing issues with government performance were highlighted by the White House Office of Management and Budget's (OMB's) little-known Performance Assessment Ratings Tool (PART), which involved a review of 399 programs conducted between 2002 and 2005. Of the programs studied, 59 were found to be "ineffective." Another 117 were assigned grades of C or D. Only 76 of the 399 programs were given A or B grades.[3] The PART evaluation programs caused a bit of an uproar and were quietly cancelled. The results, however, were consistent with other indicators of effectiveness of many programs. For instance, every year the Government Accountability Office (GAO) audits troubled government programs for waste, fraud, abuse, and mismanagement. The poorest-performing programs are included on a "High Risk List" that often becomes the subject of congressional testimony.[4]

The details of some instances of failed or troubled programs are illustrative. One prominent example is the set of problems that befell the rollout of the HealthCare.gov online marketplaces established by the Affordable Care Act ("Obamacare"). A central component of the Democrats' healthcare reform was the creation of state-level healthcare marketplaces where individuals and small businesses could browse, compare, and select among available health insurance providers' plans.[5] After the legislation's passage in 2010, the Department of Health and Human Services (HHS) and the Centers for Medicare & Medicaid Services began work on the informational technology infrastructure for HealthCare.gov. When enrollment began in October 2013, the rollout of the website was an utter disaster. Given three years of lead time, the federal government had been unable to stand up a web platform that functioned as intended, let alone was consistent with equivalent e-commerce sites in the private sector. Even worse, the government ended up spending more than $800 million for a website that took weeks to get up and running properly.[6]

The scandal of the website's launch spurred extensive reviews by the GAO and other watchdog groups, and in hindsight many of the problems should have been obvious. Over the course of years, numerous consultants and officials had issued warnings about the inadequate planning for the website's launch and the grave inefficiencies in the federal information technology acquisition process.[7] Even so, HHS charged forward with little heed to these warning signs. The result was a deeply embarrassing failure for the Obama administration, which had already suffered serious political backlash for the implementation of the healthcare law.

The troubles with HealthCare.gov were especially important because of the partisan politics surrounding Obamacare, but this is not a problem unique to Democratic administrations and policies. A more bipartisan example of failure is a long-running series of foul-ups associated with the development and acquisition of the KC-46 aerial refueling tanker.[8] Starting in the 1960s, the critical job of aerial refueling of U.S. aircraft was filled by the KC-135 tanker, the airframe of which was based on the design for the Boeing 707. By 2001, the need to replace these aircraft was evident, but the subsequent 20 years has been an illustration of exactly how important governmental needs can go unmet because of chronic failures of planning and execution. The first plan to replace the KC-135 was for the U.S. to lease 100 modified 767s from Boeing. This plan collapsed after a corruption scandal in which it came to light that the chief of Air Force acquisitions had given preferential treatment to Boeing in the contracting process, only to later be hired as a Boeing executive.

Next, in 2008 the Air Force initiated a two-year contract competition between Boeing and an Airbus–Northrup Grumman collaboration. Initially, the contract went to Boeing, only for this decision to be overturned in a bid protest as the GAO identified a series of serious deviations from the contract solicitation's stated evaluation criteria. Continuing the saga, in 2011 Boeing in fact did win the contract for the new KC-46 Pegasus tanker, but the new plane has proven to have a serious but comically simple design flaw. The new refueling boom had a set of high-tech cameras for guidance, but these cameras were subject to glare and shadows, which could lead to the boom scraping the surface of receiving aircraft. As it turns out, this is an exceptionally serious problem when aircraft surfaces are painstakingly shaped and coated with high-tech materials to make the planes stealthy and hidden from radar. After billions of dollars spent, there is some question as to whether the Air Force would have been better off dusting off the blueprints for the KC-135 and simply ordering a new batch of the venerable old tanker. In total, it took the Air Force 18 years to deliver the first pair of the new generation of aerial tanker. Napoleon conquered Europe, was defeated, and returned to nearly conquer the continent again in about the same number of years.

BLOWBACK

The term "blowback" is derived from the physical sciences, where it refers to the escape to the rear of gases formed in a boiler or the firing of a weapon. In the political realm, however, "blowback" refers to the negative repercussions of an action for those responsible for the action. The Central Intelligence Agency (CIA) began to apply the term during the 1950s to describe situations in which CIA covert military operations sparked violent acts of retaliation or led, albeit indirectly, to violent attacks against Americans sometimes years later. Today, "blowback" refers to any unintended consequence of the use of force.

One of the best-known examples of blowback is 9/11, the 2001 terror attacks in the United States.[9] The attack was carried out by a group of Islamic jihadists organized by Osama bin Laden, late leader of the al-Qaeda organization. The origins of the attacks can be traced to a decision by the United States to arm and support Afghan mujahideen fighters who opposed Soviet forces and the Soviet-backed Afghan government during the 1980s. From the American perspective, after Soviet forces entered Afghanistan in 1979, supporting the mujahideen seemed a useful and relatively inexpensive tactic in America's larger effort to weaken the Soviet Union, then America's chief geopolitical rival.

Beginning in the early 1980s, the United States armed and trained mujahideen, providing them with hundreds of millions of dollars, large quantities of small arms and ammunition, and even sophisticated Stinger anti-aircraft missiles, with which they were eventually able to destroy several hundred Soviet aircraft. The United States not only armed Afghan resistance groups, it also backed the recruitment of foreign fighters. These were mainly Muslim volunteers who traveled to Afghanistan to join the battle against the Soviets.

The most important of these was the Maktab al-Khidamat (MAK), which received funding from Pakistan and Saudi Arabia as well as the United States. The MAK recruited throughout the world, including in the United States. At any point in time the foreign fighters in Afghanistan seldom numbered more than 2,000 and they had little impact on the outcome of the fighting, but over the course of the war more than 30,000 foreign fighters gained military experience and received indoctrination. Osama bin Laden, a member of a wealthy Saudi family, was among those prominent in recruiting and training MAK volunteers. Also involved with MAK was Omar Abdel-Rahman, the "blind sheikh" who led a Brooklyn mosque and organized a 1993 bombing of the World Trade Center.

By the late 1980s, the Soviet Union (like America in 2021) concluded that its effort to subdue Afghanistan had been a costly failure, and began to withdraw its forces. Most Afghan fighters seemed content to return to peacetime pursuits. Many foreign fighters, however, hoped to put their weapons and training to use on other battlefields. Bin Laden, in particular, dreamed of using his experienced and heavily armed fighters to rid the Muslim world of Western influence and to restore it to its past glory. In 1990, when Iraqi forces invaded Kuwait, bin Laden offered the Saudi monarchy the support of his mujahideen against the Iraqis. The Saudis decided instead to seek American support and, in the First Gulf War, American forces drove the Iraqis from Kuwait and ended the threat to Saudi Arabia.

For bin Laden, as for many Muslims, the presence of American "infidel" troops in Saudi Arabia, even though invited by the Saudi government, was an affront to their religious identity. As Robert Pape has shown, the presence of foreign forces tends to spark nationalistic sentiments among native groups.[10] This is especially true when the foreigners do not share the religion and ethnicity of indigenous people. Such alien occupations, even when the foreigners do not see themselves as occupiers, seem to be among the major prequels to violence and terrorism, and this is precisely what resulted.

Bin Laden moved his operations to Sudan, where he established new training camps, and subsequently to Afghanistan. In the aftermath of the war against the Soviets, Afghanistan had been shattered into a variety of quasi-autonomous enclaves controlled by secular warlords and religious leaders. Bin Laden established a relationship with the Taliban, who controlled one such enclave. From this base, bin Laden recruited, organized, and planned, eventually deploying a team of operatives to the United States, where they hijacked four commercial airliners and used them to destroy the World Trade Center and damage the Pentagon, producing several thousand American casualties. Bin Laden hoped to provoke a massive American military response that would unite the Muslim world against America, leading to years of warfare and the establishment of a new Muslim caliphate.

Today, of course, bin Laden is dead – killed by American special operations troops. Consider, however, the heavy cost America paid and, perhaps, continues to pay in blowback that can be traced directly to the U.S. decision to intervene in the Afghan war in the early 1980s. Initially, the United States provided arms to the mujahideen, who were successfully making the Soviets pay for their foolish decision to invade Afghanistan. Blowback from this decision played a not insignificant role in the collapse of the Soviet Union. Then, however, without knowing much about them, the United States helped to arm and organize Islamic radicals, even going so far as to allow the MAK to recruit on American soil.

This decision set into motion a chain of events that included the 9/11 terror attacks, the subsequent twenty-year-long and just-ended American incursion into Afghanistan, the U.S. invasion and occupation of Iraq, and the global "War on Terror" which saw American troops in combat throughout the Middle East. The invasion of Iraq and ouster of its leader Saddam Hussein also had the effect of strengthening Iraq's rival, Iran, which has emerged as a major American adversary and poses a threat to American influence in the region. Thus, a decision to arm Afghan and foreign fighters against the Soviet Union in the 1980s had and continues to have major adverse consequences.

Blowback from the use of force is not limited to military engagements. It has domestic counterparts as well. Dr. Martin Luther King's strategy in the Civil Rights Movement is one example.[11] King intentionally and repeatedly led groups of protestors into the South to provoke local authorities, selecting the sites for his protests strategically, based on how he believed local authorities would react. For instance, King viewed Selma, Alabama as a suitable choice because he could rely on the reactionary sheriff, Jim Clark, to brutally suppress the protest for the lenses of news reporters.[12]

It is important to note that those who refrained from using force to quell domestic disturbances generally achieved better results than those who gave in to the temptation to unleash the forces at their disposal. For example, three years prior to the Selma protests, Dr. King and local black leaders organized a series of protests, boycotts, and rallies in Albany, Georgia to seek an end to segregation in that city. Albany police chief Laurie Pritchett, however, studied the Civil Rights Movement's theories and tactics and emphasized non-violent policing strategies to avoid blowback from violence.[13] The result was that the Albany protests failed to generate much publicity and produced few results. In a similar vein, while serving as president of the University of Chicago, Edward Levi refused to allow the police to interfere with student anti-Vietnam War demonstrators who had seized the school's administration building.[14] This prevented the violent clashes that had taken place at other schools. Protestors eventually left the building and were expelled from the university without much fanfare.

These examples might give pause to those who criticized Seattle, Washington mayor Jenny Durkan for refraining from using force to clear Black Lives Matter and other protestors from the so-called "Capitol Hill Autonomous Zone" they had seized in Seattle's Capitol Hill area in June 2020. The protestors had declared the six-block area to be an "autonomous zone" not subject to the city, state, or federal government. While Durkan was urged by many, including President Donald Trump, to use force, she waited until most protestors had left and several acts of violence committed within Chaz resulted in unfavorable publicity for the protestors. At this point, Durkan ordered the police to clear the remaining protestors, which they accomplished with little trouble.

The term "blowback" is often applied in settings involving violence. However, it has a homologue in more typical political activity: thermostatic public opinion. Consider the following example: a new president is elected, and in the election his or her party gains control of both chambers of Congress. Buoyed by the electoral success, even if by a narrow margin, the president is motivated by supporters to keep the promises made during the campaign. In the months that follow, the president charges forward, pushing a broad swath of changes to reshape government policy. Gradually, the public begins to sour on the administration. The promises of the campaign were only meaningful to some of the voters for the president; many just wanted to throw the previous bum out. Other citizens grow disillusioned by the new administration, seeing that the pie-in-the-sky declarations cannot be fulfilled. Yet another group of citizens appreciate the president's actions, but they desire no further movement beyond what has been accomplished. With the administration's popularity languishing, in the subsequent mid-term election the president's party suffers a debilitating defeat.

This narrative ought to sound familiar. It is, more or less, what happened in 1994, 2010, and 2018; at the time this chapter is being written, it appears very likely it will occur in 2022. The exercise of political power rarely matches the expectations of the electorate, and in a competitive political environment this leads to frequent shifts in political power. Political scientists call this "thermostatic public opinion," a term coined by researcher Christopher Wlezien in 1995, and following decades have provided robust support for this hypothesis. In Wlezien's and subsequent studies, time-series analysis of survey data has shown that once a government adopts a policy that has public support, that policy's favorability tends to decrease in the following time-period. This feedback loop has been uncovered in the contexts of government spending,[15] democratic reforms that advance counter-majoritarian principles,[16] and environmental measures,[17] to cite just a few examples. Very often, the public does not like what it gets from political leaders, even if citizens seem to have asked for those same policies.

Those endeavoring to speak truth to power are remiss if they do not warn of the danger of blowback and the reversals of public opinion. Violence has a life of its own, and whenever force is used there will almost certainly be unanticipated consequences. Relatedly, the public's appetite for change is often not as great as that of the advocates for shifts in policy. Of course, force should be the last rather than the first resort in most situations, however great the temptation to deal with antagonists once and for all. Even in more mundane political conflicts though, overextension is a serious risk that imperils the political standing of office holders. This presents a challenging balancing act for political leaders. The windows for moving policy and amassing the needed political support can be fleeting, and there is naturally an interest in jumping on such opportunities. Yet what is the value of a policy win if it means losing control over the legislative agenda and administrative state, with all the power that comes with them?

SUBOPTIMAL TRADE-OFFS

Let us now consider another unpleasant truth about the use of power. This concerns the ongoing costs of using power that are necessary to secure desired objectives. In private life, most individuals recognize that every action has a cost as well as a potential benefit. Most, indeed, seem to be "loss averse" – that is, more inclined to focus on potential risks than possible rewards.[18] In public life, however, decision-makers are less inclined to be risk-averse. Often, the risks and costs of their actions are borne by others and may not be fully realized until the distant future when current decision-makers have left the scene. The benefits of action, on the other hand, may seem current and tangible. At the very least, decision-makers can give relevant audiences the impression that they are doing something to deal with ongoing problems. Alas, however, those who endeavor to speak the truth may be forced to remind decision-makers that doing something can be far more costly than doing nothing.

The idea that the anticipated benefits of some proposed course of action should exceed their costs seems obvious, but this principle is frequently violated. One common error is a failure to consider administrative and enforcement costs. However well intentioned, every program and policy requires administration and enforcement, and in some cases the burden of administration and enforcement may outweigh the value of the program. Indeed, administration and enforcement may create new problems – a form of blowback – that render the solution worse than the problem it was intended to address. The "war on drugs" in the United States is a straightforward example.[19] The United States has spent billions of dollars in a fruitless war on narcotics, giving birth to a vast law enforcement apparatus aimed at suppressing drug trafficking. Caught up in this effort have been thousands of drug criminals. Now, as a result of overincarceration, millions of American families, predominantly black, have been disrupted, with downstream effects on household wealth and family and community integrity.[20] It is estimated that one-third of black male Americans will spend time in state or federal prison at some point in their lifetime[21] – a drag on economic mobility of an enormous portion of the American population.

Outside of law enforcement, many examples of controversies about policy trade-offs come in federal administrative law. One such example of well-intentioned policy with considerable secondary effects is environmental regulation. Clearly, environmental degradation, species loss, and climate change are serious hazards that require some degree of regulation. However, regulators must be vigilant to ensure that administrative steps required to prevent pollution do not inhibit other social and economically imperatives. In the United States, the National Environmental Policy Act (NEPA) requires that federal agencies complete a study about the environmental impacts of a regulatory action.[22] Though certainly well intentioned, NEPA has come under harsh criticism from some industry and anti-regulatory organizations for being burdensome, consuming vast resources and slowing down the regulatory process.[23] Similar critiques have emerged of federal acquisitions law. Parallel to the desirability of environmental regulation, the government clearly has a strong interest in ensuring fairness, competition, and quality when buying goods and services. However, the federal acquisitions process has become a complex legal minefield. To win a federal contract, competitors must go through a lengthy competition process. The federal government must carefully craft the requirements for goods and services as part of solicitation, and must then adhere to specific procedures and rules when determining which of the proposals submitted is the best fit for the solicitation. This process surely has benefits, but the many hoops in the process often mean that major acquisitions almost inevitably miss deadlines and become the subject of costly litigation.[24] Even with these procedures, many projects face cost overruns and result in products and services that fail to satisfy the government's requirements.

Criticisms of government actions as being illogical should not be taken at face value, because they are easily made in bad faith, motivated by a desire of special interest groups to scrap disfavored policies more than a genuine assessment of the economic and social costs of policies. Such cost–benefit analysis can be very difficult, in part because the value of policies cannot always be readily reduced to dollar values – both because the benefits are non-monetary and because of the challenge inherent to pricing the consequences of regulation. Decision-makers, however, must be able to face these concerns and incorporate them into their analysis, lest they find that a policy solution breeds more headaches than relief.

MOBILIZATION BIAS AND RENT COLLECTION

A third unfortunate truth is that the use of power is often distorted, even perverted, by mobilization biases that allow small, well-organized groups to drive decision-making to promote their own interests.[25] The basic theory of collective action outlined by Mancur Olson continues to hold true: rational self-interested people would prefer to free-ride off the work of others, and, consequently, intense organized groups often have outsized influence in policy processes.[26] Similarly, political scientist E.E. Schattschneider famously wrote that in pluralist political systems with many organized groups competing for control over the public agenda, the "heavenly chorus" of democratic actors "sings with a strong-upper class accent."[27]

Schattschneider and Olson wrote in the 1960s, but the dynamics of interest groups holding greater sway in the political process than the average citizen are as strong as ever. Washington, DC is full of lobbying organizations that are better able to communicate with lawmakers than "average" citizens, and interest groups can wield money and organizing resources that capture the attention of political and bureaucratic leaders. Such interest groups are often described as "rent seeking," in the sense that they look to shape public policy as a means to advance their policy agendas.[28] A wide range of scholarship has shown how these activities can distort public policy, but, in sum, there is an abundance of evidence to support the claim that the interests of economically advantaged Americans and powerful interest groups dominate over lower-class and political unorganized Americans.[29]

Numerous examples demonstrate the ability of interest groups to shape the policy environment in ways that are favorable to them. One example is the ethanol industry.[30] Ethanol is a petroleum product that can power internal combustion engines. In the United States, the production of ethanol using American agricultural products, primarily corn, has been heralded as a way to reduce reliance on foreign oil, and it also constitutes a valuable market for farmers' output. The ethanol industry has powerful allies in Congress coming from Midwest corn-growing states like Iowa, where, for instance, 85 percent of residents argue that the fuel source is important to the state's economy.[31] This kind of pressure from constituents is supported by a large number of lobbying groups like the Renewable Fuels Association, the National Corn Growers Association, the American Coalition for Ethanol, the National Ethanol Vehicle Coalition, Ethanol Producers and Consumers, the Illinois Corn Marketing Board, and a host of others. The end result is the ethanol industry receives billions of dollars of federal subsidies a year, making it at least somewhat competitive with other fuel sources. The problem, however, is that careful economic analysis shows that ethanol is not an especially efficient hydrocarbon fuel. Making ethanol requires 29 percent more energy than is stored in the final product, making it far less efficient to produce than other fuel sources, even if factoring in import costs.[32]

Securing subsidies is one way that rent seekers prop up preferred industries, and another is through trade protectionism. When threatened with new competitors offering superior products or lower price points, firms naturally have an interest in securing measures from the government that limit the ability of new competitors to infringe on their markets. Tariffs and licensing are two tools that governments can use on behalf of legacy industries to keep out competition. A classic example of this is steel tariffs in the United States, which are periodically proposed to keep the American steel industry alive even as cheaper international production is available. A more recent instance is related to the introduction of Tesla electrified vehicles into the car market. Tesla eschewed the traditional franchise model for car dealerships, choosing instead to market directly to customers. In response, local car dealerships – which are politically quite powerful – responded by getting state and local governments to ban the direct sale of cars and instead require that sales go through dealerships.[33] A similar process arose in cities across the United States when Airbnb, the online platform for short-term vacation rentals, began to impinge on the market for hotel rooms.[34] The hotel lobby began a multipronged national campaign at all levels of government to restrict owners' ability to rent their properties and to increase the costs of doing so.[35]

Savvy decision-makers are certainly aware of the risks of rent-seeking special interest groups influencing their decisions, and they may judge that courting such special interests as a means to hold on to political power is a good trade-off, as it allows political leaders to accomplish other policy priorities. Rent seekers can be quite cunning though, genuinely convincing leaders to take actions that inhibit innovation and lead to unnecessary and inefficient expenditures. While the voices of entrenched special interests are certainly strong, decision-makers would do well to remember that many of the analyses of the benefits of actions are skewed by those wishing to defend their own pocketbooks and constituencies. It may take time, but such chickens can come home to roost.

MORAL HAZARD

The term "moral hazard" refers to a lack of incentive to guard against risk. Policies create a moral hazard when they allow individuals or firms to take risky actions without threat to themselves. A trivially simple example is gambling with another person's money. Imagine a contract under which a wealthy thrill seeker agrees to fund a professional gambler, with the contract constructed so that the gambler would split the winnings with the thrill seeker but the gambler would bear no cost if the bet did not work out. This is obviously a foolish contract, because the gambler will eventually realize that it is in his best interest to take on increasingly risky bets. Surprisingly though, public policy parallels are not difficult to find. Many critics of the federal government's response to the 2007–08 financial crisis asserted that bailing out failed financial institutions essentially insulated those institutions from the risky securitization practices that caused the collapse.[36] In this setting, the federal government played the role of the wealthy thrill seeker that keeps funding the bets of the inveterate gamblers in the financial houses of Manhattan.

Another well-known instance of moral hazard in public policy is the Federal Direct Student Loan Program. Launched in 1965 and subsequently expanded several times, each time increasing the amount that students were permitted to borrow, the program provides federally guaranteed loans to college students and post-graduate students. Currently, millions of individuals hold student loan debt which has accumulated to $1.6 trillion.[37] To some borrowers, student loan debt can be a crushing burden. Students who borrow to earn potentially remunerative degrees in law, medicine, engineering, and the like are generally able to repay their debts without undue financial hardship. However, those who take on debt to earn degrees in, say, the humanities, often find that their incomes are barely sufficient to cover their living expenses, much less the monthly principal and interest payments on their loans.[38]

Several politicians have proposed debt forgiveness programs. As a candidate, President Biden, for example, advocated partial forgiveness of debt for all borrowers. Critics of forgiveness schemes point to the potential moral hazard loan forgiveness might create. Believing that their loans would eventually be forgiven could encourage students to take on even more debt, thus adding to their financial risk. If we take a step back, however, we see that the true moral hazard produced by the guaranteed student loan program should be seen in terms of the actions of colleges and lenders rather than students and their parents. Since the loans are federally guaranteed, lenders have no interest in looking into the credit-worthiness of borrowers or counseling borrowers not to take on more debt than the potential income from their proposed course of study can support. Currently, students are assuming debt to undertake work in such areas as surfing studies, ufology, the science of Harry Potter, Oprah Winfrey studies, and myriad topics that might be interesting but seem unlikely to be sufficiently remunerative to allow students to repay their loans.

Colleges, for their part, have every incentive to scoop up the billions of dollars in federally guaranteed loans available to students and their parents and have worked with alacrity to do so. This has taken two forms. First, since 1980 more than fourteen hundred new degree-granting institutions have been founded in the United States, secure in the knowledge that potential customers (students and parents) had the wherewithal to pay tuition. Second, rather than falling because of more competition, college tuition itself has increased sharply in the United States, more than doubling since the 1980s. The main driver of tuition increases has been the student loan program. As limits on borrowing have risen, colleges have increased their fees to take advantage of the additional dollars available to their customers.[39] Not surprisingly, through such lobby groups as the American Council on Education (ACE), the higher education industry has lobbied vigorously for increased borrowing limits. ACE and the others have claimed, rather disingenuously, that the chance to borrow more will help to make higher education more accessible to all Americans.

The complicity of America's colleges in impoverishing an entire generation of students perhaps suggests that the higher education industry should not escape unscathed from whatever solution emerges to the student loan crisis. Current proposals essentially call for taxpayer-funded relief for student debtors. But it does not seem unreasonable for colleges who benefited from the loan programs to be required to contribute to a loan forgiveness program. The legal principle would be "claw back," in which monies that have already been received as a result of some financial misdeed must be returned. In this case, America's colleges have received hundreds of billions of dollars by persuading credulous students to borrow heavily to study ufology and similar esoteric subjects. No doubt the ACE would object strenuously to this idea, but it seems a simple matter of justice for the victims of the student loan racket.

FISCAL EVASION

A final unwelcome truth to share with those in power concerns fiscal evasion. It is often the case that decision-makers trumpet the benefits of some programs while not only failing to mention the costs but hiding those costs from the public. Such fiscal evasions strip all meaning from democratic accountability and can result in untenable levels of expenditure. Budgetary chicanery occurs at the federal and state level, and both parties engage in such practices. In Washington, DC, a common tool in budgetary politics is so-called "dynamic scoring."[40] Much of Congressional legislation is ultimately about money and how it can be raised and spent. As such, an important element of the legislative process is estimating the potential costs of legislation, the impact it will have on the economy, and, ultimately, tax revenues. The challenge is that most government programs are anticipated to generate behavioral response from citizens and businesses. This raises the question of whether the results of these behavioral changes should be incorporated into budget estimates, or whether the projections should be marked to baseline behavior prior to government intervention. Presented in this way, it might seem like a "no-brainer" decision – if a government policy is likely to change behavior, then failing to incorporate those changes into projections leaves out important data and probably biases results. Even so, there are major challenges to this type of dynamic scoring, leaving open the possibility of decision-makers convincing themselves of the sunniest possible future. As the Committee for a Responsible Federal Budget has pointed out, dynamic scoring is very sensitive to economic assumptions, and economists have choices about what assumptions to make.[41] The uncertainty related with such budgetary forecasts leaves much room for politicians to cherry-pick favorable budgetary consequences for their preferred legislation. This may be the reason that the United States is under fiscal pressure, as successive waves of tax-cutting Republicans and entitlement-expanding Democrats have pushed the country's debt-to-GDP (gross domestic product) ratio consistently higher. The parties justify these decisions with forecasts that minimize the costs of their programs.

At the state level, another fiscal tool is available – the off-budget entity (OBE). State constitutions generally include balanced budget provisions and other restrictions against spending, much stronger than the limits imposed on the federal government. Even so, states have innovated around such measures, moving expenditures "off budget" and hiding their costs from citizens, legislatures, and the courts.[42] In some cases, like New York, the use of such gimmickry has made it impossible to accurately assess the fiscal condition of a state.[43]

Lawmakers are always looking for a political edge, and as the late James Buchanan observed, they are more than happy to create "fiscal illusions" as a mechanism to convince citizens that they can receive benefits at no cost.[44] Deficit spending is, thus, akin to moral hazard, pushing the costs of policies off the living tax base and requiring future policymakers and taxpayers to sort out the consequences. This might be wise politically, but it is also another example of where the use of power – even the power to deceive – comes with considerable downstream risks.

SPEAKING TRUTH

Sometimes, the government doing nothing is not an option. To offer an extreme example, if a foreign adversary is invading a nation's territory and killing citizens, it is probably incumbent on the state to take action to respond, either through negotiation or force of arms. This calls to mind the adage of sociologist Charles Tilly that "war made the state, and the state made war."[45] Armed conflict, extreme breakdowns of public order, natural disasters, and public health emergencies are all exigent circumstances that make a clear case for state action. For these reasons, competent leadership in government is essential and always will be. Perhaps the strongest use-case for expertise is such a situation. Military leaders, crisis managers, public health professionals, and other front-line emergency responders clearly have skills that government needs to be able to tap into during moments of urgency.

Many readers will argue that there are other, less urgent emergencies where there is a strong case for the state application of resources and expertise. To be sure, there is no shortage of pressing issues that face the public. Political leaders, of course, seek to satisfy that demand, and they present bold visions and grand ideas for change. No contender for office is elected to do as little as possible. As we have pointed out above, Republicans in the mold of Donald Trump seek to use the state to curb what they perceive as the cultural and economic excesses of the last 60 years. Progressives and Democrats desire to use the state to tackle issues like climate change and to reduce economic inequities associated with race. Both parties are prepared to use fiscal and monetary policy to prop up the national economic activity, keep food and fuel inexpensive, and reward their patrons in various industries.

In their efforts to achieve these objectives, political leaders naturally turn to experts to help them. Politicians want experts to make a plan to help reduce healthcare costs, or increase the stock of affordable housing, or improve the education system, or any other number of laudable (or, depending on your perspective, sinister) goals. In the modern era, there is always some kind of well-credentialed or self-described expert capable of crafting or conjuring such a solution. The problem though is that even with the best of intentions, the use of power is fraught with difficulties. Government action frequently fails. Unexpected events derail the best laid plans, and the pressures inherent in the political process may force elements of program design that are less than fully optimal.

This is a serious risk that experts should be aware of when they offer advice, either by request or on their own initiative. It is also something that expertise-oriented politicians should remember. Expertise may inform policy formulation, but with that contribution comes the risk that expertise will bear some of the risks of failure. If experts become associated with public policy ideas that fail, then the credibility of a "neutral" expertise is injured. Politicians, similarly, may find that their own subsequent appeals to experts are less persuasive to citizens. For these reasons, political decision-makers must complement their work with experts with a keen eye for the political realities of policymaking and the risks therein. Ironically, sometimes the best way to support experts might be to ignore them, and the best advice an expert can give might be to do nothing at all.

NOTES

1. Ginsberg, Benjamin. 2022. *The Imperial Presidency and American Politics: Governance by Edicts and Coups*. New York: Routledge.

2. Flyvbjerg, Bent, and Cass Sunstein. 2016. "The Principle of the Malevolent Hiding Hand; or, the Planning Fallacy Writ Large." *Social Research: An International Quarterly* 83(4): 979–1004.
3. Acosta, Alison Fraser, and Keith Miller. 2004. "Part of the Solution: The Performance Assessment Ratings Tool." Heritage Foundation. www.heritage.org/budget-and-spending/report/part-the-solution-the-performance-assessment-ratings-tool.
4. Government Accountability Office. 2021. "High Risk List." www.gao.gov/high-risk-list.
5. Government Accountability Office. 2014. "Healthcare.gov: Ineffective Planning and Oversight Practices Underscore the Need for Improved Contract Management." July 30. www.gao.gov/products/gao-14-694.
6. Baker, Sam. 2014. "Obamacare Website Has Cost $840 Million." *The Atlantic* July 30. www.theatlantic.com/politics/archive/2014/07/obamacare-website-has-cost-840-million/440478/.
7. Goldstein, Amy. 2016. "HHS Failed to Heed Many Warnings that HealthCare.gov was in Trouble." *Washington Post* February 23. www.washingtonpost.com/national/health-science/hhs-failed-to-heed-many-warnings-that-healthcaregov-was-in-trouble/2016/02/22/dd344e7c-d67e-11e5-9823-02b905009f99_story.html.
8. For an extensive report on the KC-46 acquisition with numerous links to primary materials, see Thompson, Mark, 2019, "Fill 'Er Up! Why it's Taken the Pentagon Nearly Two Decades to Buy a New Aerial Tanker," Project on Government Oversight, www.pogo.org/analysis/2019/03/fill-er-up-why-its-taken-the-pentagon-nearly-two-decades-to-buy-a-new-aerial-tanker/.
9. Johnson, Chalmers. 2004. *Blowback*, 2nd ed. New York: Holt.
10. Pape, Robert. 2005. *Dying to Win: The Strategic Logic of Suicide Terrorism*. New York: Random House.
11. Ginsberg, Benjamin. 2013. *The Value of Violence*. Amherst: Prometheus Books.
12. Garrow, David. 1986. *Bearing the Cross: Martin Luther King, Jr., and the Southern Christian Leadership Conference*. New York: Random House.
13. Id. at 209.
14. Sinhababu, Supriya. 2008. "The Sit-In: 40 Years Later." *Chicago Maroon* December 2. www.chicagomaroon.com/2008/12/02/the-sit-in-40-years-later/.
15. Wlezien, Christopher. 1995. "The Public as Thermostat: Dynamics of Preferences for Spending." *American Journal of Political Science* 39(4): 981–1000.
16. Claasen, Christopher. 2020. "In the Mood for Democracy? Democratic Support as Thermostatic Opinion." *American Political Science Review* 114(1): 36–53.
17. Johnson, Martin, Paul Brace, and Kevin Arceneaux. 2005. "Public Opinion and Dynamic Representation in the American States: The Case of Environmental Attitudes." *Social Science Quarterly* 86(1): 87–108.
18. Kahneman, Daniel. 2011. *Thinking, Fast and Slow*. New York: Farrar, Straus, and Giroux.
19. Ginsberg, Benjamin. 2007. *The American Lie: Government by the People and Other Political Fables*. Boulder, CO: Paradigm Publishers, 148–149.
20. McWhorter, John. 2011. "How the War on Drugs Is Destroying Black America." *Cato's Letter* 9(1): 1–5. www.cato.org/sites/cato.org/files/pubs/pdf/catosletterv9n1.pdf. See also Rothwell, Jonathan, 2014, "How the War on Drugs Damages Black Social Mobility," Brookings Institution September 30. www

.brookings.edu/blog/social-mobility-memos/2014/09/30/how-the-war-on-drugs-damages-black-social-mobility/.
21. *Report of the Sentencing Project to the United Nations Human Rights Committee, August 2013.* www.sentencingproject.org/wp-content/uploads/2015/12/Race-and-Justice-Shadow-Report-ICCPR.pdf.
22. For an overview of the NEPA, see "A Citizen's Guide to the NEPA: Having Your Voice Heard," Council on Environmental Quality, Executive Office of the President. https://ceq.doe.gov/docs/get-involved/Citizens_Guide_Dec07.pdf.
23. Rutzick, Mark C. 2018. "A Long and Winding Road: How the National Environmental Policy Has Become the Most Expensive and Least Effective Environmental Law in the History of the United States, and How to Fix It." Regulatory Transparency Project. October 16. https://regproject.org/paper/national-environmental-policy-act/.
24. See Savare, Matthew. 2020. "The Absurdity of Government Contracting." *Signal* June 12. www.afcea.org/content/absurdity-government-contracting.
25. Ginsberg 2007 at 126.
26. Olson, Mancur. 1965. *The Logic of Collective Action.* Cambridge, MA: Harvard University Press, 2.
27. Schattschneider, E.E. 1960. *The Semisovereign People.* New York: Holt, Rinehart and Winston, 28.
28. Lindsey, Brink, and Steven M. Teles. 2017. *The Captured Economy: How the Powerful Enrich Themselves, Slow Down Growth and Increase Inequality.* New York: Oxford University Press.
29. Gilens, Martin. 2012. *Affluence and Influence.* Princeton: Princeton University Press. Bo, Ernesto Dal. 2006. "Regulatory Capture: A Review." *Oxford Review of Economic Policy* 22(2): 203–225. See also Maisel, L. Sandy, Jeffrey M. Berry, and George C. Edwards III, eds, *The Oxford Handbook of American Political Parties and Interest Groups*, Oxford: Oxford University Press.
30. Ginsberg 2007 at 127–131.
31. Eller, Donnell. 2021. "Iowa Poll: 85% of Iowans, a 'Giant Majority,' Say Ethanol Is Critically or Fairly Important to the State's Economy." *Des Moines Register* September 24. www.desmoinesregister.com/story/news/politics/iowa-poll/2021/09/24/giant-majority-say-ethanol-important-state-economy-iowa-poll/5818848001/.
32. Pimental, David. 2001. "The Limitations of Biomass Energy." In Robert Meyers, ed., *Encyclopedia of Physical Science and Technology* (3rd ed.), Vol. 2. San Diego, CA: Academic, 159–171.
33. Craig, John, and David Madland. 2014. "How Campaign Contributions and Lobbying Can Lead to Inefficient Economic Policy." Center for American Progress. www.americanprogress.org/issues/economy/reports/2014/05/02/88917/how-campaign-contributions-and-lobbying-can-lead-to-inefficient-economic-policy/. See also Blank, Steve, 2013, "Strangling Innovation: Tesla vs. 'Rent Seekers,'" *Forbes* June 24. www.forbes.com/sites/steveblank/2013/06/24/strangling-innovation-tesla-vs-rent-seekers/?sh=753506d23981.
34. Blank 2013.
35. Benner, Katie. 2017. "Inside the Hotel Industry's Plan to Combat Airbnb." *New York Times* April 16. www.nytimes.com/2017/04/16/technology/inside-the-hotel-industrys-plan-to-combat-airbnb.html.
36. Saphir, Ann. 2020. "Seen Everywhere in the Last U.S. Crisis, Moral Hazard Is Nowhere in This One." Reuters April 12. www.reuters.com/article/us-health

-coronavirus-fed-moralhazard-an/seen-everywhere-in-last-u-s-crisis-moral-hazard-is-nowhere-in-this-one-idUSKCN21U0GV.
37. Federal Reserve Bank of New York. Center for Microeconomic Data. www.newyorkfed.org/microeconomics/topics/student-debt.
38. Korn, Melissa, and Andrea Fuller. 2021. "'Financially Hobbled for Life': the Elite Master's Degrees That Don't Pay Off." *Wall Street Journal*, July 8. www.wsj.com/articles/financially-hobbled-for-life-the-elite-masters-degrees-that-dont-pay-off-11625752773.
39. Gordon, Grey, and Aaron Hedlund. 2016. *Accounting for the Rise in College Tuition*. National Bureau of Economic Research Working Paper 21967, February. www.nber.org/papers/w21967.
40. Lynch, Megan S., and Jane G. Gravelle. 2021. *Dynamic Scoring in the Congressional Budget Process*. Congressional Research Service. https://sgp.fas.org/crs/misc/R46233.pdf.
41. Committee for a Responsible Federal Budget. 2014. "Understanding Dynamic Scoring." www.crfb.org/papers/report-understanding-dynamic-scoring.
42. Bachner, Jennifer, and Benjamin Ginsberg. 2021. *America's State Governments: A Critical Look at Disconnected Democracies.* New York: Routledge.
43. Confessore, Nicholas. 2010. "Grab Bag of Gimmickry Hides State Deficit." *New York Times* April 6. https://cityroom.blogs.nytimes.com/2010/04/06/albany-accounting-hides-deficit-size-comptroller-says/.
44. Buchanan, James M. 1999. "Public Finance in Democratic Process: Fiscal Institutions and Individual Choice." In *The Collected Works of James Buchanan*, Vol. 4. New York: Liberty Fund.
45. Tilly, Charles. 1985. "War Making and State Making as Organized Crime." In Peter Evans et al., eds, *Bringing the State Back In*. Cambridge, UK: Cambridge University Press, 169–187.

6. Expertise and political conflict: a macroscopic view

In the last chapter, we described some of the problems associated with bringing expertise to bear on policy problems. In short, many times policy solutions fail, and experts and political decision-makers are often well served to keep this reality in mind. However, there is a second, perhaps even greater, risk that we have not addressed. In a macro political sense, beyond discrete societal challenges, expertise can amplify social conflict. It is a substrate upon which societal clashes grow. In this chapter, we describe how this happens in several parts. We first review a few of the roles that experts play in macro political struggles, then we provide a deeper look at the role of expertise in major conflicts in Western society.

To begin to explain what we mean, first consider the public image that experts have fostered. Experts, perhaps scientists in particular, often view themselves and prefer to be viewed as politically neutral truth tellers. During the COVID-19 pandemic, for example, the news media often characterized public health physicians as apolitical experts seeking to speak unwelcome truths to politically motivated governors and presidents, and these selfsame experts undoubtedly agreed with this characterization. In the world of international affairs, the American national security and intelligence communities value their relationships with both the Republican and Democratic parties, sticking to an old approach that "politics stops at the water's edge." For some disciplines, like engineering or materials sciences, it is comparatively straightforward to argue that there is no Democratic or Republican approach to building a road.[1] More broadly, many experts outside of government work for universities and think tanks that are organized as 501(c)(3) organizations whose tax-exempt status requires that the institutions not engage in partisan politics.

Yet, seen from a somewhat larger perspective, even if individual experts and methodologies of expertise are insulated from politics, expertise is seldom a neutral force. Instead, expertise and experts should be understood as political cudgels that political actors can pick up and wield in societal struggles with far-reaching implications for the distribution of power. However innocent in their personal motivations, experts who do public-facing research are offering a resource to politicians who look to advance their own agendas. This is to say nothing of the potential for experts themselves to push forward their own political preferences.

THE ROLES OF EXPERTS IN POLITICAL CONFLICT

In battles between competing political and social forces, experts play four major roles. They help to develop narratives and counter narratives, they interpret events in such a way as to exemplify the appropriate narrative, they work to discredit the experts who might validate opposing points of view, and, finally, they develop solutions to manifest problems in a manner consistent with or in furtherance of the goals of the forces with which they are associated. We examine each of these roles in turn.

Development of narratives

First, experts help to develop narratives and counternarratives that respond to new political or social realities. In the worst case, this could lead to the distortion of empirical truth, wrapped in the guise of traditional academic norms. At other times, a narrative created by experts hews more closely to reality, but the narrative may be picked up and co-opted for the purpose of a political agenda.

An example where rewriting an older narrative has a positive outcome is the correction of the history of the post-Civil War Reconstruction in the United States. During the 1870s and 1880s, northern business elites were anxious to end political strife in the South and resume their restructuring of the American economy.[2] This required bringing an end to radical Reconstruction. To achieve this purpose, business elites were able to secure the cooperation of both political parties and major segments of the media, and to identify and publicize the work of sympathetic historians. Accordingly, during the late 19th century many media accounts and histories of Reconstruction began to emphasize the sufferings and struggles of southern whites in the wake of the Civil War. In the 1940s and 1950s, historians including John Hope Franklin and others began to confront this odious mythology, revealing the truth behind the development of the southern apartheid state.[3] As historian Eric Foner has noted, the old history of Reconstruction reflected and was designed to reinforce one set of political understandings, and the revised history was intended to comport with and reinforce contemporary understandings born during the Civil Rights era.[4] In this instance, the new history was surely more accurate than the previous, but the motivation for the new research was at least in part to disrupt the political order. This can also be seen in contemporary historical accounts of slavery such as the *New York Times* 1619 Project, which places the brutal enslavement of Africans at the very center of American history. We will return to this issue below.

To provide a second instance of how experts have reimagined previously held understandings about history and social theory, consider the development of the field of peace studies. For centuries, practitioners and scholars of international relations deemed war to be a natural part of every international system. From Thucydides through Machiavelli and Hobbes and to the early 20th century, a "realist" theory of international relations developed that described international politics as about groups, self-interest, and power competition. From these assumptions, a basic expectation of realist thought is that international politics is likely to be characterized by conflict.[5]

When wars were fought by relatively small armies and nobles, international strategy based on the principle that conflict was inherent to interstate relations was a tolerable paradigm. While many wars were indeed terrible, they were a sustainable part of political life. Over the course of the 19th and 20th century though, the advent of industrialized total warfare and, later, weapons of mass destruction dramatically increased the stakes of international conflict. When the stakes of realism became too high to accept that war was unavoidable, scholars of international relations began to develop alternative visions of foreign affairs that recast the role of conflict. After World War II, scholars in the newly emerging field of "peace studies" began to argue that peace arose not through war or burgeoning economic co-dependence, but rather that peace requires strong international institutions, the submergence of purely national interests and the development of transnational peacekeeping forces. Free trade, they point out, is often a mask for exploitation of the poor by the rich. Many peace studies experts especially criticize capitalism, most notably American capitalism, and neoliberalism for generating aggressive tendencies and international tensions and rivalries.[6]

Interpretation of Events

A second role played by experts is the interpretation of events in a manner that reinforces the kinds of narrative or counternarratives we describe above. At one time, priests interpreted events, including celestial phenomena, to explain the way in which they reflected or comported with God's will and ongoing political struggles. Today, academics, scientists, and, very often, media pundits strive to interpret events in light of the dominant elite narratives. To liberal pundits and academic experts, a tragic, if statistically rare, school shooting is compelling evidence for an anti-gun narrative while for conservative pundits and academic experts a tragic, albeit very rare, murder committed by an undocumented immigrant demonstrates the importance of immigration restriction. In 2020, the appalling killing of George Floyd, a black man, by a white Minneapolis, Minnesota police officer became an example used by pundits to bolster an ongoing narrative of police brutality towards African Americans. This event sparked weeks of protests and demands for the reorganization, if not outright abolition, of police forces in the United States.

Where appropriate events do not occur spontaneously, competing social forces may employ public relations experts to devise and organize the examples needed to allow sympathetic media pundits and academic experts to drive home the truth of a particular narrative. Advocates often intentionally frame events to create political "facts" for public consumption.[7] A famous example is the 1956 photo of Rosa Parks refusing to yield her bus seat to a white man. Parks was a trained National Association for the Advancement of Colored People (NAACP) organizer, selected for this role especially for her suitability as a symbol for the Civil Rights Movement. The "angry white man" behind her was placed there by *Look* magazine photographers.[8]

A dramatic event, properly portrayed, can attract the attention of the mass media, and inspire stories and photos that ultimately influence the attitudes of millions of readers and viewers. As the Parks case suggests, leaders of the Civil Rights Movement were especially adept at the use of the news media and sympathetic pundits to gain widespread popular support for their cause. Dr. Martin Luther King, in particular, learned to use television to illustrate to northern audiences that the southern Jim Crow system was brutal, evil, and fundamentally un-American.[9] In his efforts, Dr. King was supported by an alliance of northern white liberals, segments of the business community, and important elements of the national news media themselves.[10] The media not only saw a powerful story, but also saw an opportunity to castigate the conservative coalition of southern Democrats and right-wing Republicans that had tormented journalists and broadcasters over their alleged Communist ties during the 1940s and 1950s. This alliance gave Dr. King extraordinarily good access to the nation's television screens and helped him to sway public opinion in favor of his cause.

Outside the domain of racial progress, the tendency to interpret events as consistent with larger narratives is readily apparent in the climate change discourse. Faced with the difficulty of convincing the public of the reality of climate change with complex and slow climatological processes, for example, environmental scientists have relied on interpreting a variety of seemingly disparate events such as global temperature fluctuations, changes in the size and consistency of the polar ice caps, and severe hurricane and fire seasons as evidence supporting their narrative. Climate advocates then take the further step of connecting these events with unfettered industrial activity that results in environmental degradation and potential disastrous changes in the earth's climate.

Discrediting Rival Experts

A third role played by experts is discrediting rival experts. The ability of scientists to discredit the knowledge of priests played a part in the victory of the bourgeoisie over the crown and aristocracy. For a contemporary example, let us consider the case of LGBT+ rights. Today gay rights, including same-sex marriage, are recognized by the courts; queer characters are common in the media; celebrities, politicians, and members of the clergy acknowledge their sexual and gender identities. Cities around the United States celebrate Pride Week every year with parades and other public events. It is hard to remember that not so many years ago same-sex relationships were illegal in most states. Homosexuality was deemed a perversion by most religious groups and was viewed as a mental disorder by the psychiatric profession. For many years, the *Diagnostic and Statistical Manual of Psychiatric Disorders* (DSM) classified homosexuality as a mental illness that psychiatrists sought to cure.

The gay rights movement began with street protests in the 1960s, and during the 1970s and 1980s developed a sophisticated and well-funded campaign of lobbying, electoral mobilization, and litigation led by the Human Rights Campaign (HRC), an organization that currently boasts some three million supporters, and Lambda Legal, one of several organizations that pursue what has been a very successful strategy of litigation to attack statutes and practices deemed to discriminate against LGBT+ persons. HRC and other gay rights advocates are politically aligned with other political groups that view themselves as seeking major changes in American politics and institutions in a "progressive" coalition, to which we shall return below.

One of the most important early steps in the legitimation of homosexuality involved a battle within the psychiatric profession between rival groups of experts. Even though Alfred Kinsey's work during the 1940s and 1950s had concluded that homosexuality was a normal variant of human sexuality, until the 1970s most psychiatrists took the position that homosexuality was a type of paraphilia, a generally pejorative term used to characterize deviant sexual interests and mental disorders. During the 1960s, however, dissident psychiatrists, including Richard Green, Judd Marmor, and Robert Stoller took issue with this characterization and launched a campaign to change the way in which the psychiatric profession regarded differences in sexual preferences. This campaign consisted of scholarly studies, articles in medical journals, and papers presented to scientific conferences challenging the classification of homosexuality as a disorder. They called upon the psychiatric profession to recognize the validity of Kinsey's studies and recognize homosexuality as simply another variation in sexual interest. Sigmund Freud himself was quoted as writing that homosexuality was "nothing to be ashamed of, no vice, no degradation, it cannot be classified as an illness."[11] During the 1970s, gay and lesbian psychiatrists organized their own caucus within the American Psychiatric Association (APA) to advocate for the declassification of homosexuality as a mental disorder.

Gradually, the dissident experts carried the day and discredited those psychiatrists who supported the traditional view of homosexuality. In 1973, after a tumultuous debate at the Honolulu annual APA meeting, homosexuality was removed from the DSM and officially recognized by the psychiatric profession as a normal variant of human sexuality.[12] This victory for the dissidents was an important step forward for the LGBT+ community and a victory for the larger progressive coalition whose banner has come to include gay rights.

One element of the progressive critique of contemporary America is the alleged falsity of the core American narrative claiming that any person can succeed through individual initiative and hard work. Demonstrating the pervasiveness of racism, sexism, and homophobia undermines the idea of success through individual effort and helps progressives to pave the way for a more statist approach to economic and social issues. In this way, the psychiatrists who pointed out that homosexuals had been unfairly stigmatized were also pointing to a flaw in America's governing narrative. We shall return to this matter below.

Develop Narrative-Consistent Solutions to Problems

Finally, experts are needed to solve problems in a manner that is consistent with the goals and overall ideology of political leaders. Any given problem is likely to lend itself to a variety of different solutions. In the political realm, experts are called upon to solve problems in a manner consistent with the larger goals and world view of political leaders and the forces they represent. To give a dramatic example, in the run-up to the Civil War the matter of southern secession might have been resolved by compromise, as many in the North favored, or by acceding to southern demands, an idea that also had supporters. However, Lincoln, the Republican leadership, and the political forces they represented sought the complete and unconditional defeat of the South. Accordingly, for Lincoln, only one Union general offered the right advice. Grant – whose nickname had become "Unconditional Surrender" Grant – was the Union general whose military tactics, though productive of enormous casualties, promised to deliver total victory rather than stalemate and compromise. The Civil War might have been ended in other ways, but Lincoln was set on a solution that matched his own beliefs about the sanctity of the union and severity of breaking it.

The need to solve problems in ways that align with larger world views is readily apparent in many domains of American domestic policy today. As we described above, Franklin Roosevelt and his New Dealers were interested in expanding the role of the national government and the Keynesians, among economic experts, offered advice that entailed a larger governmental role. In large degree, this Roosevelt-ian impulse still drives much of American domestic policymaking on the Democratic side. After taking office in 2021 with, in a surprise, control of both chambers of Congress, many observers wondered whether Joe Biden would be a new Roosevelt and have a similarly impactful administration that expanded the federal safety net. Some Democratic politicians in favor of greater government spending have gone so far as to embrace a post-Keynesian economic theory, "modern monetary theory," that justifies enormous government deficits as a tool to achieve full employment.[13]

By contrast, when Republicans espouse similar goals, they tend to pursue them with a different set of policy tools. A prime example here is the domestic policy vision of former Speaker of the House Paul Ryan. Ryan – a self-described conservative policy wonk – tried to make fighting poverty a priority for the Republican Party, attempting to co-opt a traditional issue of the Democratic Party. His methods for achieving this goal, however, were much different. With the support of free market organizations like the American Enterprise Institute, U.S. Chamber of Commerce, and Business Roundtable, Ryan's preferred approach for reducing poverty was to institute more stringent work requirements for government support programs and to shift responsibility for providing social services to nonprofit organizations and local governments.[14] Thus, we might say that the value of advice is measured by its consistency with the ideas of those receiving it.

EXPERTISE IN MACRO POLITICAL STRUGGLES

The strategies we have described above go beyond any particular policy domain. Through the creation, defense, application, and critique of theoretical narratives, experts have an important role in significant societal changes. While not always at the vanguard of social change, experts are often the midwives in these processes. In every society, competing political and social forces employ experts to formulate and bolster narratives that justify their own claims to power and privilege while undermining those of their opponents. While this formulation may sound sterile, the practical effects can be dramatic.

This pattern is evident from the very beginnings of recorded history. In the pre-modern world, a variety of experts, including priests, shamans, legal scholars, philosophers, and historians, propounded and wove narratives celebrating kings and aristocrats and even interpreted history as the interplay between gods and heroic rulers. Religious experts were important pillars of the political order, ordained by the relevant gods as experts. In Europe, Catholic priests were the experts who explained political events in light of and in support of this narrative. Rulers ruled by the grace of God and were removed only when they lost God's favor. Priestly experts might also be consulted on ordinary matters of health, agriculture, animal husbandry, personal disputes, and sundry other matters. Adverse events, including pestilence, drought, and famine were punishments meted out by God that might be mitigated by prayer and sacrifice – also organized and directed by priestly experts.

When the European bourgeoisie attacked and sought to displace the power of the crown and aristocracy, new types of experts were identified and touted – some from the new universities – to promulgate and promote a counter-narrative. Liberal philosophers and economists wrote treatises explaining the value of liberty and capitalism. New historians deemphasized the roles of royal and aristocratic heroes and began to look, instead, to the importance of such bourgeois activities as industry, trade, and commerce as the driving forces in human affairs. The bourgeoisie also extolled the work of scientific experts who sought to discredit the priests who had trumpeted the virtues of the established order. These scientific experts demonstrated that their learning and techniques could offer better answers than the priests' religious doctrines to questions ranging from health care, silviculture, agriculture, and indeed the basic workings of the universe. By besting religious explanations, science helped the bourgeoisie to defeat the political institutions supported by religion. And, even within the realm of religion, the bourgeoisie supported new "Protestant" religious experts who affirmed the importance of the bourgeois values of frugality, hard work, and worldly success and preached that these offered better evidence of God's grace than even the most solemn attestations of any Catholic priest.[15] Eventually, the march of liberal ideas espoused by the expert class ended the monarchies, ushered in the capitalist economic system, and created the modern world. Much of the effort and costs of this were borne by politically active citizens and organizations, but a group of experts provided a narrative for this process.

Justice and Expertise in the United States

The process of transformation in the West, which moved society from the feudal to neoliberal systems, has not ended. Expertise marches on, and social and political movements continue to find support, and targets, in experts' output. This pattern is currently playing out again in the United States as controversy continues to boil over the role of race in American history and the broader social structure. The Black Lives Matter protests following the murder of George Floyd in the summer of 2020 were an important event in this movement, and clearly those protests suggested a widespread popular consciousness of the continued racism in the United States. However, it is important to interpret these events in context, especially with respect to the role of experts in framing this social conflict. In short, the essential political contention in the United States today is as much about the role of experts in society, and the narratives they create, as it is about any public policy issue. The political conflict over Black Lives Matter originates, at its foundation, from the long history of the West using criminal sanctions and incarceration to solve its domestic problems.[16] This pattern goes back to the time of the Framers. In Western Europe, commonly used criminal sanctions included public flogging, branding, mutilation, and dismemberment as well as cruel and degrading forms of execution.[17] Severe corporal punishments including public hangings were also common in the American colonies and, after independence, were not immediately ended by the 8th Amendment's prohibition of cruel and unusual forms of punishment.[18] In the nearly 250 years since the American Revolution though, there has been a significant divergence between the United States and its Western counterparts. Whereas many European countries now have comparatively progressive criminal justice and social welfare services, the United States has a far less extensive welfare state and a much more extensive criminal justice system. With respect to the number of citizens who are incarcerated or have a history of incarceration, America's only rivals are authoritarian states like China and Russia.

The reasons for this divergence are related to how experts interpreted the pressing social problems facing the state in Europe and the United States, and how national narratives developed in these two political settings. In Europe, much of the 19th century was about urban class conflict. In the pre-modern era, popular protests in the West, while feared, were not seen as major threats to the social and political order. A bit of property might be destroyed and the mob's ringleaders ultimately hanged, but generally, as historian Eric Hobsbawm put it, rioting rarely caused political problems.[19] By the 19th century, though, the attitudes of the upper classes towards popular disorder had changed substantially. In Europe, the bourgeois perceived a growing threat of violence and disorder stemming from the existence of an enormous and restive urban proletariat.[20] The process of industrialization, urban migration, and the proletarianization of the lower orders had been associated with heightened mass resistance, class conflict, political disorder, and radical political agitation by movements endeavoring to build popular bases of support. These came to include enormous socialist and labor movements that sought to take control of European governments through a mix of agitation and electioneering. This popular unrest and disorder posed a "lethal threat," according to historian Karl Polanyi,[21] to the functioning of delicate market economies than had been the case before. In the 19th century, rioting that would hardly have caused a ripple one hundred years earlier would lead to breakdowns in the delivery of food and other goods, disruptions in trade and manufactures, and stock market collapses. The bourgeoisie of nineteenth-century London, Paris, and Berlin lived in constant fear of crime and violence. Perhaps the old country gentry had felt safe on their isolated and guarded estates, but the urban bourgeoisie lived in proximity to, and often among, those whom they feared. During this period, Parisians developed an "overwhelming preoccupation with crime as one of their normal daily worries," writes social historian Louis Chevalier.[22]

Faced with these developments, European experts began to construct an answer as to what to do about this emerging threat. Indeed, controlling the dangerous urban crowd became a major theme of the new European discipline of sociology as manifested in such works as Gustave Le Bon's 1892 masterpiece *Psychologie des foules*. Of course, European states did expand and centralize their police forces in response to fears of social instability,[23] but they also turned to various forms of public welfare – supplementing the stick with the carrot. European nations do have a long history of providing some degree of poor relief,[24] but this was supplanted by comprehensive systems of public welfare. The modern European welfare state was born in the early 1880s as Bismarck's Germany adopted systems of sickness and accident insurance and old-age pensions for workers. Bismarck's main goal in advancing a program of what was then called "state socialism," was to undermine workers' support for radical political movements and to cement working-class allegiance to the monarch and the state. "My idea," Bismarck explained, "was to bribe the working classes, or shall I say, to win them over, to regard the state as a social institution existing for their sake and interested in their welfare."[25] The perceived success of the German experiment spawned numerous imitators.[26] By the beginning of World War II, most Western European regimes had at least laid the foundations of their modern welfare states, some explicitly along German lines and others seeking improvements on the German model.

This European history of the use of violence by the state and the role of the state in public welfare should be contrasted with the American case. In the 19th century, when European urban life was incubating Marxist thought, the United States was still in an expansionist phase of conquering a vast continental empire. In 1800, no city in North America was among the world's hundred largest cities.[27] By contrast, London, Paris, and other European centers were among the largest in the world and European population density was far greater. While American cities certainly grew quickly and shared many of the same problems as those in Europe, for dominant Anglo Americans their identity remained less tied to urban problems. While Western Europe was devising social programs to quiet crime and disorder, America's state and federal authorities continued to rely upon the police baton and the prison to maintain social order, especially so in the South, where police maintained the apartheid state through violence. The basic effect of having "wide open spaces" and allowing for the racial domination of black Americans through violence was to allow the carceral state in the United States to sink its tap roots into the nation's political economy and its consciousness. Today, many Americans reflexively link crime with punishment. In fact, upholding the social order through criminal sanctions remains critical to the balance of political power in the United States, made evident through the extreme resistance that criminal justice advocates face when trying to reduce overincarceration and return voting rights to convicted felons in many states.

As European academics developed social theories centered on economics and class in the 19th century, in the 20th century American social theorists began to articulate a critique of U.S. political institutions based on race. Many Americans, black and white, have correctly pointed out throughout American history that attitudes about race are a central inconsistency in American political life. To give just one example, in 1852 Frederick Douglass said in a famous oration, "The existence of slavery in this country brands your republicanism as a sham, your humanity as a base pretence, and your Christianity as a lie."[28] For decades, advocates for racial justice echoed similar sentiments, up to and including prominent leaders of the Civil Rights Movement in the 1960s. A notable shift began to occur, however, in the 1970s, when legal scholars like Derrick Bell, Kimberlé Crenshaw, and others began to describe a mode of legal analysis that aimed at describing how racism figured into the development of the law and broader political institutions.[29] Perhaps most importantly, critical race theorists advance the idea that law is not an objective practice but rather is part of sustaining social injustice. The enduring reliance of the United States on criminal sanctions to enforce the social order, and injustices that exist within it, is a prime example.

In isolation, critical race theory (CRT) is an academic legal theory, mostly of interest to researchers within the scholarly community. Outside of the legal academe, however, the post-1960s era in the United States has seen tremendous growth in efforts to enhance equity and inclusion in many sectors of American society. It is commonplace for large corporations and universities in the United States to employ at least one high-ranking officer charged with integrating women and historically underrepresented minorities into their organizations and customer base. The effectiveness of these measures is perhaps debatable, but the energy behind these efforts at least in name is undeniable. Today, equity and inclusion are critical pillars of progressive politics, and rooting out systemic racism is one of the stated objectives of most leaders in the Democratic party.

Put simply, belief in a future multiracial democracy and the rooting out of racially designed institutions is a threat to older theories of the social order in the United States. Rather than sustaining the social and racial order through criminal sanctions, progressive politics today demands a complete re-evaluation of the nature of that social order and motivations behind it. Thus, when protestors call for defunding police, they are attacking a set of institutions that are central to the contemporary American state and to the underside of the neoliberal narrative. While it might be a good thing that experts have formulated an intellectual narrative for this movement, it comes with a price. Just as experts have devised competing narratives in the past, conservative politicians and opposing experts have found a focusing idea themselves by attacking CRT. In 2021, conservative organizations converged on a strategy of elevating CRT from the status of little-known legal theory, casting it instead as a broader, insidious effort to undermine the foundations of "traditional American values." The was made explicit in a tweet from Chris Rufo, a fellow at the Manhattan Institute who is broadly credited with devising this tactic. Rufo wrote:

> "Critical race theory" has been a master-signifier for left-wing racialist ideology for the past two decades. Our innovation was to promote the signifier to the public and load it with negative connotations. That's how politics works in a postmodern society. Deal with it.[30]

Rufo's unapologetic and remarkably forthright disclosure encapsulates the role of the "expert" in many American political conflicts today. Examining American society, academic experts sifted through events and articulated a narrative that bound those events together. The policy implications of that narrative, some of them actively being implemented, threaten a broader societal order. In response, counter-experts and politicians pounce upon that narrative and articulate their own alternative account. At each stage, expertise is central to larger social conflicts. In some sense, expertise and its application in public policy debates and social debates has a destabilizing effect. A well-constructed critique of the dominant narrative, once in the hands of activists and political decision-makers, can be a dangerous thing.

GRIST FOR THE MILL

Experts are sometimes seen as politically neutral individuals who seek to speak truth to power. Yet, expertise and experts are seldom neutral in practice. Expertise is a weapon in political struggle and experts are foot soldiers in larger battles. When scientists demonstrated that their understanding of the natural world was superior to that of the priests, they struck a blow for the bourgeoisie against the aristocracy and church. Today, experts holding opposing sets of views on such matters as climate change, gender, racism, and the value of lockdowns to combat disease are locked into a severe political conflict, with some calling for the censoring or "cancelling" of critics of their narrative.

This all-or-nothing conflict over expertise in service of political agendas has potentially severe consequences. Whether experts choose to admit it or not, many issues in American society operate in shades of gray, either in terms of the origins of problems or in terms of the appropriate responses to emerging problems or the righting of past and continuing wrongs. When two sides have experts at their disposal who abandon norms of intellectual debate and embrace a Manichean approach to discourse, it does little to support citizens' competence and trust in broader political and social institutions. Some citizens react by withdrawing from democracy entirely, and others react by deepening their allegiance to a set of well-resourced and well-developed political and media ecosystems. The result, unfortunately, is a downward spiral of reliance on expertise that risks compounding existing political and social divisions, cloaked in citations to preferred prophets.

NOTES

1. This echoes the old adage attributed to Mayor Fiorello La Guardia of New York City that "There is no Democratic or Republican way of cleaning the streets."
2. Bensel, Richard Franklin. 1991. *Yankee Leviathan*. New York: Cambridge University Press.
3. Franklin, John Hope. 2010. *From Slavery to Freedom*, 9th ed. New York: McGraw-Hill.
4. Foner, Eric. 1988. *Reconstruction: America's Unfinished Revolution*. New York: Harper, xxii.
5. For an overview of realist theory, see Wohlforth, William C., 2008, "Realism," in Christian Reus-Smith and Duncan Snidal, eds, *The Oxford Handbook of International Relations*, Oxford: Oxford University Press, 131–149.
6. Barash, David, and Charles Webel. 2017. *Peace and Conflict Studies*. New York: SAGE.
7. Ginsberg, Benjamin. 2007. *The American Lie: Government by the People and Other Political Fables*. Boulder, CO: Paradigm Publishers, 53.
8. Applebome, Peter. 2005. "The Man Behind Rosa Parks." *New York Times*, December 7. www.nytimes.com/2005/12/07/nyregion/the-man-behind-rosa-parks.html.
9. Garrow, David. 1986. *Bearing the Cross*. New York: Random House.
10. Ginsberg, Benjamin. 2013. *The Value of Violence*. Amherst: Prometheus Books.
11. Lewes, Kenneth. 1988. *The Psychoanalytic Theory of Male Homosexuality*. New York: New American Library, 48.
12. Rosen, David. 2013. "How Homosexuality Became Normalized." *Counterpunch* December 6. www.counterpunch.org/2013/12/06/how-homosexuality-became-normalized/.
13. Kelton, Stephanie. 2020. *The Deficit Myth: Modern Monetary Theory and the Birth of the People's Economy*. New York: Public Affairs.
14. Campbell, Alexia Fernandez. 2016. "The Conservative Plan to Tackle Poverty." *The Atlantic* December 15. www.theatlantic.com/business/archive/2016/12/paul-ryan-poverty/510836/.
15. Weber, Max. 2008. *The Protestant Ethic and the Spirit of Capitalism*. New York: Norton Critical Edition.
16. Whitman, James Q. 2003. *Harsh Justice*. New York: Oxford University Press.
17. Id. at 27.

18. The 8th Amendment was eventually applied to the states in 1962.
19. Hobsbawm, Eric J. 1965. *Primitive Rebels*. New York: Norton.
20. Melossi, Dario. 2008. *Controlling Crime, Controlling Society*. Malden: Polity Press, 40.
21. Polanyi, Karl. 2001. *The Great Transformation: The Political and Economic Origins of Our Time*. Boston, MA: Beacon Press, 186.
22. Chevalier, Louis. 1973. *Laboring Classes and Dangerous Classes*. Princeton: Princeton University Press, 1.
23. Bailey, David H. 1975. "The Police and Political Development in Europe." In Charles Tilly, ed., *The Formation of National States in Western Europe*. Princeton: Princeton University Press, 341.
24. Francis Fox Piven and Richard A. Cloward. 1971. *Regulating the Poor*. New York. Random House: 8.
25. Dawson, William H. 1894. *Germany and the Germans*. New York: D. Appleton and Company, 347.
26. Weyland, Kurt. 2008. "Toward a New Theory of Institutional Change." *World Politics* 60(2): 281–314.
27. Satterthwaite, David. 2020. "The World's Largest Cities from 1800 to 2020, and Beyond." International Institute for Environment and Development. www.iied.org/worlds-100-largest-cities-1800-2020-beyond.
28. Douglass, Frederick. 1852. "What to the Slave Is the Fourth of July?" Teaching American History. https://teachingamericanhistory.org/document/what-to-the-slave-is-the-fourth-of-july/.
29. For an overview of critical race theory, see West, Janel, 2021, "A Lesson on Critical Race Theory," American Bar Association, www.americanbar.org/groups/crsj/publications/human_rights_magazine_home/civil-rights-reimagining-policing/a-lesson-on-critical-race-theory/.
30. Rufo, Christopher. 2021. Tweet. November 23. https://twitter.com/realchrisrufo/status/1463192368983670784?s=20.

7. Convincing the powerful of the truth

Many Americans acquire an impression of decision-making derived from television, movies, and edited viral videos. Because of the nature of mass entertainment, the decisions presented frequently are in military, law enforcement, emergency response, or medical settings. In such worlds, a key decision-maker, in the heat of the moment, may call upon senior staffers for information that will inform a critical decision. Do we launch the missile? Must we end treatment for the critically injured patient? A few advisers may provide conflicting advice or an impassioned plea for justice, and the decision-maker renders a judgment – cue the music.

Another popular view of decision-making is portrayed in legislative settings. Likely the most famous fictional moment in legislative politics is Mr. Smith's impassioned filibuster defending himself against charges of corruption and praising American democracy in the classic film *Mr. Smith Goes to Washington*. Similarly, dramatic floor speeches or committee hearings are the highlights of coverage of Congress, state legislatures, and municipal government. Legislators call upon their colleagues to seek common ground, serve greater purposes, and see the substantive merits of proposed legislation.

Appealing though they are, these vignettes are simply not representative of most political and governmental processes in the United States, or around the world for that matter. To be sure, dramatic events occasionally happen, but the vast majority of the time, politics is a slow, uncomfortable interaction of politicians strategically shaping and responding to public opinion, while a group of professionalized experts attempt to introduce preferred policies into the political system. When dramatic events do occur, like pandemics, high-visibility violence, or climate disaster, most often experts have already raised the alarm about such possibilities but have been unable to motivate any actions to head them off.

Given this unsatisfying mode of operation, it is little wonder that trust in government has plummeted in the United States. As technological and scientific progress has offered more insight into how to solve problems, it has cut against trust in two directions. For citizens who are sympathetic to increasing state power and motivated to right the wrongs of today's world, a government that does not appear responsive to those impulses is almost beyond comprehension. Yet many expert-driven responses to actions are dependent on increasing exercise of state power, which to other members in the political community is an invasion into the realm of private decision-making and jeopardizes their own position in the social order.

It would be useful if experts and politicians could find an optimal strategy in this context, one that responded to policy problems while minimizing the risks of harming or alienating the population, somehow manufacturing consensus around some set of policy solutions. Unfortunately, though, we are forced to be honest and report that, like scenes we described above, this remains more hopeful than realistic. The basic issue is that experts and decision-makers have multiple fundamental goals that conflict with each other, and they also place differing values on the outcomes of policies. Beyond that, experts face serious problems with communicating with the public and shoring up their own credibility.

INCOMPATIBILITIES BETWEEN EXPERTS AND POLICYMAKERS

Aggregated Versus Distributed Benefits

An important dimension of the differences between experts and decision-makers is that the two groups assess the benefits of proposed actions through dissimilar lenses. To experts, evaluating the desirability of a particular policy proposal is a process in which the likely *overall* costs of a particular course of action are weighed against the likely social benefits of the action. To policymakers, however, the *distribution* of costs and benefits matters more than the aggregate costs and benefits. In other words, who gets what is likely to be more important than the overall value of a program.

This difference is especially clear in the realm of tax policy. To an economist, taxes are designed to raise revenue, to direct private sector activity into avenues desired by the government, to promote economic stability, and for other purposes.[1] Proposed tax laws can be evaluated in terms of their ability to accomplish these goals. For policymakers, however, whatever else it might accomplish, a proper tax policy rewards supporters and punishes opponents. For example, the Tax Cuts and Jobs Act of 2017 (TCJA), developed by the Trump administration and passed by congressional Republicans, lowered income tax rates for the Republican Party's higher-income supporters, and lowered the corporate tax rate from 35 percent to 21 percent. Between 2017 and 2018, corporations paid 22.4 percent less income tax. The total value of refunds issued by the Internal Revenue Service to businesses also increased by 33.8 percent. Low- and middle-income taxpayers received few, if any benefits from the TCJA.[2] The Trump administration, like most other administrations, was concerned with the distributional effects of its tax program, not the aggregate effects. The Biden administration is seeking to reverse these effects by increasing taxes for higher-income wage earners and corporations.

Timeliness

Beyond how they value differently the outcomes of a policy action, experts and policymakers often have different conceptions of timeliness. To experts, timeliness is generally problem-driven. Experts understand that policies take time to formulate, implement, evaluate, and adjust. The speed at which they work to develop solutions is governed by the nature and severity of the problem. Experts may also carefully track the mounting costs of problems as well as the compounding costs of corrective actions. For policymakers, on the other hand, timeliness is politically driven – governed by the electoral calendar, the budget cycle, and other political considerations.

In some instances, experts and decision-makers do march in lock step. In 2020, President Trump was anxious to be able to announce a vaccine that could prevent COVID-19 before the November elections. Experts were less concerned about the election but were eager to produce a vaccine as soon as possible. Trump, to be sure, forced federal agencies to accelerate the regulatory process and authorize the emergency use of an experimental vaccine to meet his political deadline. Trump also pressured experts to minimize his political liabilities by downplaying the severity of the pandemic.[3] Some experts had misgivings about the rapidity with which vaccines were approved but, fortunately, the vaccines resulting from what the Trump administration called "Operation Warp Speed" turned out to be safe and effective.

In other cases, though, electoral considerations have driven policymakers to ignore expert opinion with disastrous results. For example, in 1980 President Jimmy Carter ignored the opinions of most military advisers and the vehement objections of Secretary of State Cyrus Vance when he ordered a mission to rescue fifty-two Americans held hostage by the Iranians.[4] Carter feared that the ongoing hostage crisis would be fatal to his chances for reelection, and gambled that the mission might succeed. The hostage rescue mission was a dismal failure and helped ensure Carter's defeat at the polls later in the year. The differences between "political time" and "policy time" are readily apparent in the debate over gun control, in which the crisis seems exceptionally urgent with each mass shooting, and every day without greater gun control is another day where the body count increases. When asked when he planned to address the matter of gun control in the wake of another mass shooting, President Biden replied that timeliness had to be understood as a political matter.[5]

Endogenous versus Exogenous Criteria

Both experts and decision-makers hope new policies will solve problems, but it is important to distinguish how the communities differ in terms of identifying those problems and solutions to them. Experts tend to evaluate proposed policies based on exogenous criteria; for example, will they solve problems in the real world. Decision-makers, on the other hand, tend to be concerned with endogenous factors – that is, how will a proposed solution affect them. Politicians perceive problems through the lens of maintaining their own political power, in the sense that underlying social problems are co-extensive with the political problems they create. Bureaucracies too share this tendency. Government agencies are most interested in expert advice that is consistent with their established priorities and procedures, such that it will not threaten the existing distribution of power within the bureaucracy. We saw this tendency in Chapter 4, where government agencies showed a consistent tendency to seek out advice that supports the institutional missions and culture.

Public Perceptions of Expertise and Democratic Responsiveness

There is another factor that makes it difficult for experts to collaborate with political decision-makers. Put simply, experts are very poor at educating the public about their findings and recommendations. This blame is shared to some extent between the community of researchers and scholars and the broader citizenry. As we have described, all humans possess cognitive biases that make it difficult for them to learn about issues outside of their immediate area of experience. Motivated reasoning and flawed heuristics cause people to look for information that conforms with their pre-existing beliefs, makes them draw conclusions from inappropriate small samples, and causes them to react out of envy and jealousy when their own position in society is threatened.[6] When an expert tries to describe a new problem or perhaps a new solution to that problem, everyday people are often predisposed towards skepticism if not hostility towards information that might not conform with their own viewpoints or might imply the need for material sacrifice on their part. All these innate challenges precede whatever effects there may be of biased news media and other public figures who seek to persuade the public to oppose findings or measures that are counter to other extant institutional interests.

From this starting point, experts who want to communicate with the public, presumably to help guide public decision-making, start from a serious disadvantage. Concerns about science communication have created a huge scholarly corpus aimed at understanding how science communication processes work and what, if anything, scientists can do to help reach citizens and overcome the obstacles to creating shared public knowledge.[7] These efforts are commendable and certainly ought to continue, but clearly there is much work to be done. If there is a single example of the shortcomings of science communication, it must be the public response to the COVID-19 vaccines that were introduced in the winter of 2020. Despite essentially universal consensus from the public health community about the jab's safety and effectiveness, a significant portion of the population in the United States simply refuses to get vaccinated. If there is a clearer instance of disconnect between the expert consensus and public opinion, it is hard to imagine.

The role of experts in the policymaking process must also be viewed in the context of the wider loss of confidence in political institutions in the United States. In a pre-pandemic poll from 2019, the Pew Research Center found that 67 percent of American adults have "not too much confidence" or "no confidence at all" in the federal government, and many other surveys have found similar results.[8] This is nearly an inversion from the 1950s and 1960s, when more than two-thirds of Americans trusted government to do what is right just about always or most of the time.[9] These survey results are complex; it matters how questions about trust are asked, and trust varies significantly across different actors in American government and across partisan groups. However, the central finding that social and political trust in the United States are at historic lows is unavoidable. Scientists may be relatively more trustworthy than other public figures, but the elected officials and bureaucracies, who make political decisions and implement policies based on expert advice, are as poorly perceived as ever. Expertly crafted solutions to public policy problems might be ideal, but if they must be filtered through governments in which citizens have little confidence, expertise reaches a limit in terms of what it can achieve.

Even as experts increase their technical ability, American politics faces a major crisis of legitimacy, and political interests are served by elite actors egging on this distrust. In response, there is a burgeoning and promising conversation that has begun about reforms to American democracy that might enhance political responsiveness and restore public confidence.[10] Perhaps modifications to electoral systems or other political reforms like eliminating partisan gerrymandering would be helpful. Of course, experts in politics are happy to provide suggestions. Until the situation improves, though, the skepticism that many citizens hold towards government will color their perceptions of bureaucratic, centrally administered public policy solutions.

TOWARDS A MORE REALISTIC UNDERSTANDING OF TRUTH AND POWER

Despite their frequent incompatibility, experts sometimes manage to persuade intransigent policymakers and the public to accept unpleasant truths. As we have seen, during periods of crisis, desperate decision-makers may be compelled to reach out to experts whom they had previously rebuffed. Thus, Stalin had been wont to murder experts who disagreed with his military plans, but he proved more willing to listen as the German army approached Moscow. Shrewd experts, moreover, may be able to structure their advice in ways that appeal to policymakers' parochial interests. In the 1980s, for example, America's military bureaucracies resisted the idea of creating a special operations command to coordinate counter-insurgency and other low-intensity conflict missions. The Pentagon's leaders thought such forces undermined the conventional warfare missions upon which their own power and service budgets were based. A number of experts, however, including Defense Department officials Noel Koch and Lynn Rylander, strongly supported the idea of a special operations command, and were able to organize its command structure in such a way that the conventional services saw it as enhancing rather than competing with their missions and career ladders.[11] Finally, experts are sometimes able to ally themselves with interest groups and mount campaigns that bring pressure upon decision-makers to listen to them. After decades of political and media pressure led by scientific experts, for example, all but the most willfully ignorant decision-makers are now compelled to acknowledge the realities of climate change. While climate policy is still resisted by a vocal and pivotal minority, there is no longer room for debate over its reality.

As these examples suggest though, speaking truth to power is possible but is no easy matter. There is a wide literature that concerns how experts might be able to best build partnerships with decision-makers, towards the goal of better policy. At minimum, this requires understanding policymakers' political needs and interests and can entail a high level of organization and political acumen on the part of policymakers themselves. Speaking truth to power effectively requires salesmanship as much as scientific excellence.[12] Obviously, experts should be sensitive to policymakers' political priorities and personal perspectives. However, we are forced to conclude that while such steps may increase the probability that an expert will become a successful policy entrepreneur, they are far from being sufficient. Expert advice is both an input and output of the political process, a strategically manufactured pill that can be difficult to swallow for whatever political decision-makers command the state at a given time. Experts should be prepared for failure when they offer policymakers advice the latter do not wish to hear.

America's 19th-century Progressives believed that reliance on experts would depoliticize governance and policymaking and lead to a society in which science, technology, education, and economic development would improve the human condition. As we noted in Chapter 1, Walter Lippman called for a cadre of technocrats to advise and guide political decision-makers. That tradition continues today, with public policy schools around the country producing graduates who are skilled in policy formulation, cost–benefit analysis, and forecasting. We do not mean through our work to gainsay the value of this kind of analysis and advocacy. Given the choice, policies ought to be justifiable based on rigorous evidence-gathering. Our goal, however, throughout this book has been to show that the idea that experts can stand outside politics and arrive at politically neutral, technocratic decisions is quite naïve. Expertise can be a counterweight to irrational policy decisions, to the extent that it provides political ammunition for opposition decision-makers. Unfortunately though, the increasing prevalence of expertise in policymaking has served to slow down and complicate these processes, not to streamline them. It supports the status quo as much as moves it, which frustrates reformers, and it makes policy decisions less understandable to citizens.

One can imagine a world where experts have a greater hand in political decision-making. A stronger civic culture, greater tolerance, and more skillful science communication could all be helpful in this regard. Further, governmental policies that either expand or retract the state have greater legitimacy if there is a shared, empirically supported expectation about the tradeoffs involved. However, in the ongoing effort to create that understanding, truth is a servant of power at least as much as it is a corrective to it.

NOTES

1. Musgrave, Richard A. 1959. *The Theory of Public Finance*. New York: McGraw-Hill.
2. Public Law 115–97. U.S. Statutes at Large, 131 Stat. 2054.
3. Diamond, Dan. 2021. "Trump Officials Say Response Was Worse than Public Knew." *Washington Post* March 29. www.washingtonpost.com/health/2021/03/29/trump-officials-tell-all-coronavirus-response/.
4. Brinkley, Douglas. 2002. "The Lives They Lived: Out of the Loop." *New York Times Magazine* December 29. www.nytimes.com/2002/12/29/magazine/the-lives-they-lived-out-of-the-loop.html.
5. Viser, Matt, and Annie Linskey. 2021. "'The Art of the Possible': Biden Lays Out Pragmatic Vision for His Presidency." *Washington Post* March 26. www.washingtonpost.com/politics/biden-pragmatic-agenda/2021/03/25/d8fec310-8da2-11eb-a730-1b4ed9656258_story.html.
6. Kuklinski, James, and Paul Quirk. 2001. "Conceptual Foundations of Citizen Competence." *Political Behavior* 23(3): 285–311.
7. Among many sources, see for a recent review Baruch Fischhoff, 2019, "Evaluating Science Communication," *Proceedings of the National Academy of Sciences of the United States of America* 116(16): 7470–7675, www.pnas.org/content/116/16/7670. A second review is Michael F. Weigold, 2001, "Communicating Science: A Review of the Literature," *Science Communication* 23(2): 164–193.
8. Rainie, Lee, Scott Keeter, and Andrew Perrin. 2019. "Trust and Distrust in America." Pew Research Center. www.pewresearch.org/politics/2019/07/22/trust-and-distrust-in-america/.

9. Pew Research Center. 2021. "Public Trust in Government: 1958–2021." www.pewresearch.org/politics/2021/05/17/public-trust-in-government-1958-2021/.
10. Drutman, Lee. 2020. *Breaking the Two-Party Doom Loop: The Case for Multiparty Democracy in America*. Oxford: Oxford University Press.
11. Department of Defense. N.d. *History of the United States Special Operations Command*. https://fas.org/irp/agency/dod/socom/2007history.pdf.
12. Cairney, Paul. 2018. "Three Habits of Successful Policy Entrepreneurs." *Policy & Politics* 46(2): 199–215.

Index

9/11 terror attacks 13, 88–90

Abdel-Rahman, Omar 89
ACS *see* Affordable Care Act
action, preference for 62–3
actuarial models 24
administrative costs trade-offs 92
Administrative Procedure Act 77
advisory committees 1, 69–76
advocacy organizations 18
Affordable Care Act (ACS) 77–8, 87
Afghan war 88–90
aggregated benefits 118–19
AI *see* artificial intelligence
Air Force KC-46 initiative 87–8
algorithmic bias 40–41
American Civil War 55–7, 108
appeasement policy 59
artificial intelligence (AI) 16, 30–31, 33
Austin, Lloyd 71

balance principle 72
Balla, Steven J. 72
bank failures 47
Banks, Nathaniel 56
behavioral economics 28–30
Bell, Derrick 113
beta personality 29, 30, 50, 54–63, 64
Biden, Joe 15, 70–71, 78–9, 96, 109, 119
big data 31, 34
"Big Five" personality model 61–2
bin Laden, Osama 88–90
birds in the bush 12, 14–15
Bismarck, Otto von 112
Black Lives Matter movement 91, 110–111
black swans 12–14, 15, 22, 47
Blair, Robert A. 34–5, 42
blowback 88–92
Bossie, David 71
Bright, Rick 6

Brown, Mark B. 72
Buchanan, James 98
Budenny, Semyon 50
budgetary politics 9–10, 97–8
Bueno de Mesquita, Bruce 31, 36
bureaucracy 68–84
 democracy and 4–5
 disaster prediction 36–7
 endogenous/exogenous factors 120
 governance 2
 power of 80–81
 resistance to change 38
bureaucratic agencies 1, 69–76
bureaucratic expertise 76–80
bureaucratic leaders, conflict with political leaders 68
Bush, George W. 5
Butler, Benjamin 56

Carlson, Tucker 46
Carter, Jimmy 11–12, 119
Cassandras 12, 24, 41
causal inference 25, 26, 38
Centers for Disease Control (CDC) 6, 13, 68–9, 79
Central Intelligence Agency (CIA) 88
Chamberlain, Neville 60
Chevalier, Louis 112
Churchill, Winston 54, 57–61, 64
CIA (Central Intelligence Agency) 88
Civil Rights Movement 90, 104, 106, 113
civil wars 34–5, 42, 55–7, 104, 108
Clark, Jim 90
class conflict 111–12
Clay, William L. 70
climate change 14–15, 19, 106, 122
Clinton, Bill 70–71
cognitive biases 120
cognitive entrenchment 47, 50–52, 54–61
cognitive styles, experts 29
cognitive systems, judgment 28

125

Cohen, Eliot A. 51
Cold War 5
collective action theory 94
conflict forecasting 34–5
Congress 3, 9–10, 69–70, 72, 77–8, 85
Congressional Budget Office (CBO) 9–10
cost-benefit analysis 93, 118
Coughlin, Charles 50, 54
counternarratives 104, 105, 110
COVID-19 pandemic 6, 7, 13, 22, 68–9
  bureaucratic conflict 78–9
  policymaking 119
  political neutrality 103
  public health 17–18, 22, 46
  science communication 121
Crenshaw, Kimberlé 113
criminal justice 111, 113
crises
  decision-making and 43–67, 121–2
  experts on 63–4
  political interests 2
critical race theory (CRT) 113–14
Cuban Missile Crisis 43–5
Cuomo, Andrew 7

debt forgiveness programs 96
decision-making
  conflict with expertise 1–23, 118–20
  crises and 43–67, 121–2
  legislative settings 117
  perpetual betas and 61–3
  risks of power 85, 92
"deep learning" 31
Defense Advanced Research Projects Agency (DARPA) 34
deficit spending 98
demand for expert advice 7–19
democracy 3–7
Democratic Party 15, 72, 78, 85, 99
democratic responsiveness 120–121
Department of Defense (DoD) committees 71
DeSantis, Ron 6
Dewey, John 5
Diamond, Jared 43
disaster prediction 36–7, 39
distributed benefits 118–19
diversity of advice 16–18
Douglass, Frederick 113

Ducey, Doug 7
Durkan, Jenny 91
dynamic scoring 97–8

EBPM *see* evidence-based policymaking
economic depressions 47–50
economic forecasts 9–10
education program evaluation 9
election campaigns 27, 39–40, 91, 119
emergency responses 99
endogenous factors 120
enforcement costs trade-offs 92–3
Environmental Protection Agency (EPA) 70–71, 78
environmental regulation 93
EPA *see* Environmental Protection Agency
epistemic closure 10
ethanol industry 94–5
evidence-based policymaking (EBPM) 8–9, 72, 81
exogenous factors 120
expertise
  democracy and 3–7
  emergency responses 99
  filtering 68–9
  oversupply of 16–19
  politics and 79–80, 103–16
  public perceptions of 120–121
  supply and demand 7–19
  in war 98, 122
experts
  cognitive styles 29
  conflict with decision-makers 1–23, 118–20
  on crisis 63–4
  distrust of 5–7
  policymakers versus 118–23
  risks of power 99

FACA *see* Federal Advisory Committee Act
FACs (federal advisory committees) 69–76
failure
  consequences of 12, 18, 51, 58
  planning for 86–8
  positive effects 61, 63–4
federal acquisitions law 93

Index

federal administrative law 93
Federal Advisory Committee Act (FACA) 69–76, 78–9, 81, 83
federal advisory committees (FACs) 69–76
Federal Direct Student Loan Program 96–7
federal government, size/scope 5–6
Feinstein, Brian D. 72
financial crises 13–14, 37–8, 96
fiscal evasion 97–8
Floyd, George 105–6, 110
Flyvbjerg, Bent 86
Foner, Eric 104
Food and Drug Administration (FDA) 79
forecasting 30–35
   see also prediction
Foundations for Evidence-Based Policymaking Act 8
"fox-style" reasoning 29–30, 61–2
Franklin, Benjamin 3, 16
Franklin, John H. 104
Fremont, John C. 56
Freud, Sigmund 107

game theory 30–31, 35–6
gay rights movement 107–8
General Services Administration 26, 69
golden geese 12, 15–16
Gooch, John 51
Good Judgment Project 29, 61
"Google Trends" offering (GT) 33–4
Gorsuch, Neil 80
government, trust in 117, 121
Government Accountability Office (GAO) 86–7
government agencies 1, 37, 40, 68–84, 120
government-sponsored enterprises (GSEs) 13
grant proposals, government agencies 1
Grant, Ulysses S. 54, 56–7, 60–61, 63–4, 108
Great Depression 5, 47–50
Green, Richard 107
Gruber, Marion 79
Gulf War 89
gun control policies 119

Halleck, Henry 57
Harris, Seymour 47
Hassan, Maggie 70
HealthCare.gov website 87
"hedgehog-style" reasoning 29, 61, 62, 64
heedless decision-makers 10–12
Hemel, Daniel J. 72
herd mentality 17
Hitler, Adolf 10, 59–60
Hobbes, Thomas 105
Hobsbawm, Eric 111
homosexuality 107–8
Hoover, Herbert 47–8
Human Rights Campaign (HRC) 107
Hussein, Saddam 90

individualistic culture 4
inference 25–7, 38
influenza pandemic 46
institutional cultures 68, 120
institutional reforms 64
institutionalization 77, 78–9
Integrated Conflict Early Warning Systems (ICEWS) 34–5
intelligence services 52
interest groups 72–3, 75, 78, 93, 94–5
international relations 105
interpretation 25–7, 105–6
intolerance of uncertainty scale (IUS) 62–3
Iraq 89, 90
Israeli military campaigns 51–2

Jackson, Andrew 4, 6, 45
"Jacksonian democracy" 4
Japanese military campaigns 52–4
Jefferson, Thomas 3, 4, 16
Jenner, Edward 16
Johnson, Lyndon 5
Joint Legislative Oversight Committee (JLOC) 9
judges' political preferences 80
judgment 28–30
justice 110–114

Kahneman, Daniel 28–9, 30
KC-46 aerial refueling tanker 87–8
Kennedy, John F. 43–5

Keynes, John M. 48–50, 54, 57, 60–61, 64
  The Economic Consequences of the Peace 48
  General Theory 49
  The Means to Prosperity 49
Keynesianism 47–50, 109
King, Martin L. 90, 106
Kinsey, Alfred 107
Knightian uncertainty 37–8
Koch, Noel 122
Krause, Phil 79

Ladapo, Joseph 6
Lavalle, Nye 14
law enforcement 92–3
  see also police forces
"law of small numbers" 28
leadership personality traits 64
Lee, Robert E. 64
legal theory, race 113–14
legislators, roles of 3, 117
Levi, Edward 90
Lewandowski, Corey 71
Lewis, Michael 12–13
LGBT+ rights 107–8
Lincoln, Abraham 55, 56–7, 108
Lippman, Walter 3, 5, 122
liquidationism 47–50
lobbying organizations 94–5
Long, Huey 49, 50, 54
"loss aversion" 92

MacArthur, Douglas 12
Machiavelli, Niccolò 105
machine learning 31, 34, 36
macro politics 103–16
Mahan, Alfred T. 52
Maktab al-Khidamat (MAK) 89, 90
markets for ideas 7–19
Marmor, Judd 107
Marxism 112
maximin principle 38
May, Ernest R. 11
McClellan, George 56–7
McClernand, John 56
McGann, James G. 18
McNamara, Robert 43–4
Mellon, Andrew 47–8

Miller, Chris 71, 73
Minsky, Marvin 16
mobilization bias 94–5
moral hazard 95–7
Morgenthau, Hans J. 59
motivated information search 8–10, 120
Murphy, Eddie 20

"Napoleonic Idea" 52, 56
narcissistic personality disorder 11
narratives 104–5, 108–9, 114
Nash, John 30
National Environmental Policy Act (NEPA) 93
Nazism 59–60, 64
Neustadt, Richard E. 11
neutral perspective, politics 3, 103, 114
New Deal 77, 79, 108–9
Nixon, Richard 11
non-delegation doctrine 79–80

Obama, Barack 15, 77–8, 87
Obamacare 77–8, 87
off-budget entity (OBE) 98
Office of Evaluation Sciences (OES) 26
Office of Management and Budget (OMB) 9–10, 70, 86
Olson, Floyd 49, 54
Olson, Mancur 94
OMB *see* Office of Management and Budget
openness-to-experience factor 61–2
oversupply of advice 16–19

Pape, Robert 89
Papert, Seymour 16
paraphilia 107
Paris agreement 15
Parks, Rosa 106
peace studies 105
Performance Assessment Ratings Tool (PART) 86
perpetual betas 29, 30, 50, 54–63, 64
Perry, Rick 72
personality traits 11, 50, 61–3, 64
"planning fallacy" 29, 86–8
Polanyi, Karl 111
police forces 90–91, 106, 112–13
policymakers versus experts 118–23

political conflict, expertise 103–16
political neutrality 3, 103, 114
politicization of expertise 76–80
Portman, Rob 70
Post, Jerrold M. 11
prediction 24–42, 43
predictive analytics 26, 39–41
predictive modeling 31, 33–4
Pritchett, Laurie 90
problem solving 108–9
program evaluation 8, 9
Progressive movement 4–5, 18, 99, 122
prospect theory 28
protest actions 33–4, 35, 110–111
public health 17–18, 22, 46
public relations experts 106
punishment 111, 113

racial conflict 110–111, 112–13
Raines, Franklin 14
randomized controlled trials 25–6
Reagan, Ronald 5
"realist" theory 105
regression modeling 32–3
religious experts 109–10
rent seeking 94–5
representative members, committees 73–4
Republican Party 15, 72–3, 99, 109
republicanism 3
Rescorla, Rick 13
riots 111
risk aversion 28, 92
risk of using power 85–102
rivalry, experts 107–8
Roosevelt, Franklin D. 5, 48, 49, 77, 79, 108–9
Rosenblatt, Frank 16
Rostenkowski, Dan 36
Rufo, Chris 114
Ryan, Paul 109
Rylander, Lynn 122

Sambanis, Nicholas 34–5, 42
Schattschneider, Elmer E. 94
Schumpeter, Joseph 47
science communication 120–121
scientific expertise 45–6, 110
scientific inference 26

shirking and sabotage 78
Silver, Nate 24
slavery 104–5, 113
smallpox vaccination 15–16
social order 112–13
Soviet Union 10–11, 43–5, 50–52, 88–90
"special government employees" 73
Stalin, Joseph 10–11, 50–51, 122
"statistical machine learning" 31
statistical models 30, 36
"statistical significance" 38
Stein, Herbert 49
Stoller, Robert 107
stress, effects of 44–5
student loan programs 96–7
Sunstein, Cass 37–8, 86
"superforecasters" 30
"supervised machine learning" 31–2
supply and demand, expert advice 7–19

Taleb, Nassim N. 12–13
tariffs 95
Tax Cuts and Jobs Act (TCJA) 118
tax policy 9, 76, 97–8, 103, 118–19
technical expertise 45–6
Tetlock, Philip 29–30, 50, 57, 61–2
thermostatic public opinion 91
think tanks 1, 18–19, 45
Thinking, Fast and Slow (TFS) systems 28
Thomas, Clarence 80
Thucydides 43, 51, 105
Tilly, Charles 98
timeliness concept 119
Timoneda, Joan 33
Timoshenko, Semyon 50
Townsend, Charles 50, 54
trade-offs, suboptimal 92–3
trade protectionism 95
Truman, Harry 12
Trump, Donald 5–8, 11, 15, 39–40, 69–72, 77–8, 85, 91, 99, 118–19
trust in government 117, 121
Tversky, Amos 28, 29
Twain, Mark 55

uncertainty 37–8, 62–3
universities, expertise 1, 45

Vance, Cyrus 119
Vannikov, Boris 11
Voroshilov, Kliment 50

Walensky, Rochelle 79
war 43, 50–57, 98, 122
"war on drugs" 92–3
welfare state 111, 112
Wibbels, Erik 33
Williams, Thomas H. 57
Wlezien, Christopher 91

World War I 22, 38, 48, 58
World War II 5, 39, 43, 105, 112
Wright, John R. 72

Yamamoto, Admiral 52–4, 61

Zeira, Eliyahu 52
Zhukov, Georgi 51
Zinke, Ryan 71